THE
PLAN A
MOM
IN A PLAN B WORLD

THE
PLAN A
MOM
IN A PLAN B WORLD

Raising Faithful Kids
in a Flawed World

DEBBIE TAYLOR WILLIAMS

LEAFWOOD
PUBLISHERS

The Plan A Mom in a Plan B World

Raising Faithful Kids in a Flawed World

Copyright 2011 by Debbie Taylor Williams

ISBN 978-0-89112-281-4

Printed in the United States of America

The names of some individuals mentioned this book have been changed to protect their privacy.

Cover design by Jason Barnes
Interior text design by Sandy Armstrong

1626 Campus Court
Abilene, Texas 79601
1-877-816-4455 toll free

For current information about all Leafwood titles, visit our Web site:
www.leafwoodpublishers.com

11 12 13 14 15 16 / 7 6 5 4 3 2 1

In Memory

of my mother, Bernice Taylor,
who taught me to love Jesus.

Dedicated to

Keith's and my children, Taylor Williams and Lauren Williams Spalding,
and their spouses, Ali and Chris. I love you and am so proud of you.

Contents

PREFACE

I had the opportunity to be with both of my children when they prayed to receive Christ. Taylor, our son, who is now thirty, married to Ali, and practicing law, was ten when he received Christ. My husband and I had hosted an overnight water-ski fellowship. Mike Davidson, the youth minister, had led the youth group in worship on Friday night, and Taylor, as usual, was in the midst of the activity. After a full day of skiing on Saturday, the teens piled into church vans and headed home. After everyone left, Taylor came into our bedroom. I could tell something was on his mind. "Do you remember last night, when we were singing and Mike was talking about asking forgiveness for our sins? I want to pray and ask Jesus to forgive my sins." No more precious words could have fallen on my ears. "Why don't we kneel and pray right now, Taylor," I encouraged him. Recalling that moment brings tears to my eyes. My sweet son told Jesus he was sorry for his sins and asked Jesus to forgive him and come into his heart. That day, Taylor's soul was sealed for eternity in heaven. "Thank You, Father," I cried to God from every part of my being.

Our daughter, Lauren, is now twenty-seven, married to Chris, has one son and another on the way, and works part time for my ministry. She grew up with even more opportunities to learn about Christ than Taylor did: in addition to hearing about Jesus from Keith and me, she was also influenced by her brother's commitment to Christ.

I recall one evening, while telling her good night, her conversation turned serious. She asked if there really was a devil and hell. She asked about God, Jesus, and forgiveness. The next afternoon, Lauren asked me, if someone wanted to become a Christian, how they would do it? As I was telling her what such a person could pray, she knelt beside me and prayed. Again, my heart soared. My spirit, in reverence and awe, thanked God for bringing Lauren to saving faith at such a young age. To this day, my heart swells with gratitude. God, how good, how great You are!

Is our children's salvation enough, though? Once they're saved, can we check their souls off our To Do list? Can we say, "Whew! That's done!" Hardly. Our children are growing up in a culture where violence, sexual intercourse outside of marriage, oral sex, sexting, immodesty, drugs, and disrespect are the norm in the television shows they watch, the music they listen to, and the books they read. Peer pressure is powerful, and without parents to whom they can confide; who lead by example; who pray for their children and provide love, discipline, and consistency; our kids have little chance of standing against what Paul describes in Ephesians 6 as forces of darkness.

Whatever hope we parents have for our children must begin with taking a close look, not at them, but within ourselves.

ACKNOWLEDGMENTS

When I wrote *The Plan A Woman in a Plan B World*, I wrote my acknowledgements first. I already knew to whom I wanted to express appreciation. This time I'm writing them last, and while some people I'm acknowledging are the same, others are different.

My hubby is the best with a capital B! Yes, I know writers shouldn't overuse exclamation points, but this hubby deserves them. Over thirty-five years of marriage and he still loves me, reads everything I write, proofs it, and tells me when I need to replace that Lauren had a "chunk of wood" in her foot with "large splinter." I love you, Keith.

Our children are gifts from God! (Can I keep using exclamation points?) So are their spouses. And, need I tell you that our grandson is going to be Abraham, Noah, Moses, and David wrapped into one, with a touch of Paul and Peter? Taylor and Ali, Lauren and Chris, thank you for being the incredible children and Christians you are. Thank you for your prayers, insights, words of encouragement, responsiveness to my parenting, putting up with your silly mama, loving me in spite of all the ways I goofed up, of which I don't have enough space to detail. You are my joy, and I love you more than words can express.

Linda McConnico, my sister, might as well have been my coauthor. Almost every day I called her with a question, asked her to read a chapter, or called with a prayer request. The same holds true for my sister Vicki Tate. God has blessed me with two sweet, godly, wise sisters. Thank you, Linda and Vicki, for your love and prayers. You mean more to me than I can convey.

To my board of directors, friends, and prayer team, who advise and pray for me ... thank you. I will spend eternity hugging your necks! You literally saw me through the last chapter with your prayers.

Gary Myers, Leonard Allen, Bill Jensen, Jason Barnes, you men are great. It's an honor to do Kingdom work with you.

Dawn Brandon, thank you for once again making my book a better read. It is a pleasure to have you as my editor. I truly enjoy your sense of humor.

Thank you to each of the moms who shared her story with me for this book. I learn from you. You exhort me to be a better mother and person. I'm confident that, in heaven, the readers you've touched through your testimony will seek you out to celebrate the truths they learned from you.

Father, Son, and Holy Spirit, in awe and reverence I present to You the work that I pray is not of my hands, but Yours. Transform the moms who read these pages through the power of Your Word. Increase the fruit of Your Spirit in them. Make them shining vessels of Your glory. Turn their children's hearts toward home, and fix their children's eyes on You. Raise up through these moms a generation who doesn't go the way of the world but cautiously examines everything to see if it's not just good, but godly. To You be the honor, power, and glory. In Christ's name, amen.

Welcome!

Most little girls grow up playing with baby dolls. In our pretend Plan A world, we are Plan A mothers. We feed our dolls bottles of pretend milk, change their diapers, and dress them. We may even tuck them into a doll bed at night or cradle them in our arms as we fall asleep.

However, in case you've never noticed, dolls are quite cooperative. They don't talk back unless you pull their string. They cry and wet on demand, not in the middle of the night. They lie still while you change their diaper rather than flail their arms and legs. When our dolls are older and go to pretend school, they sit quietly while we teach them. They make good grades. When we carry them around by their hair or ankle, they don't mind. Nor do they complain if we ignore them for days. So, just as we grow up expecting to marry Prince Charming and live happily ever after, we also expect to be great mothers who raise perfect children—ones who are loving, cooperative, healthy, athletic, brilliantly accomplished, and who love Jesus.

The truth is, there are no perfect children or mothers, and we live in anything but a perfect world. When we go "into labor," it's far more than the five to twenty hours we spend pushing a little one from the birth canal into the world. Our "labor," or work, actually never ends. And although after birth our children live on the outside of our physical bodies, they forever live in our hearts.

If you love and adore your child and are convinced that you're a perfect mother and your child and the world are perfect, you're reading the wrong book. Put it down quickly.

On the other hand, if you love and adore your child but sometimes wish you could carry him or her around by the ankle—or you wish you could wiggle your nose and magically make the world perfect—then this is the book for you.

What has been your Plan B parenting experience? Is your toddler more controlling than compliant? Is your son a bookworm instead of an athlete? Does your adult daughter refuse to talk to you? Has a debilitating illness struck you or your child?

After working in Christian ministry to women for over thirty-five years, I can assure you that you're not the only mother who sometimes feels overwhelmed, discouraged, and at your wits' end. As we face parenting challenges and disappointments, it's understandable that we wonder . . .

How can I raise my children to be not just good but godly?

What do I need to guard against so that I don't fail my children?

How can I encourage my adult children in their walk with God?

In each chapter of this book, you'll find the following three sections geared toward helping you find answers to those questions.

Live Out Loud

In this section we'll explore how to **live out your faith in front of your children**. If we want to do more than raise good kids—if we want to raise godly ones—and if we want to encourage our adult children in their walk with God, we must model Christianity so that it is "caught" as well as taught. They must see that Christianity is more than a sermon and prayer at church: it's a relationship with Jesus lived by the power of His Spirit within us. They must see we have a different mind-set than the world; that our renewed minds influence our decisions and the way we relate to God and others.

The Live Out Loud section highlights areas where we might falter in living out our faith. Why might we falter? Several reasons. First, we live in a Plan B world and are influenced by the world's thoughts and behavior. Second, we may have been raised in a home where less-than-godly parenting skills were practiced. Finally, we have a sin nature that Satan knows how to target, especially under the stress of parenting.

Through stories of women in the Bible and of contemporary women, we'll examine some Plan B parenting practices and attitudes—I call them land mines—that undermine what we're trying to accomplish as godly, Plan A moms. The goal is to prayerfully identify and defuse any of these "land mines" that are sabotaging your Plan A mothering efforts.

Love Out Loud

Mothers benefit from discussing parenting practices with one other, so in this section you'll find helpful **mom-to-mom discussion starters**. Titus 2:3–8 instructs older women to encourage younger ones to love their husbands and children. The Love Out Loud section has scripturally based discussion questions for moms of all ages.

Whether you get together with one friend or a group, this section will encourage and support your efforts to model Christ to your children.

Laugh Out Loud: Enjoy the Lighter Side of Life

Sometimes moms get so busy doing "life" that we leave little time for ourselves. Plan A moms may feel worried and burdened. Proverbs 17:22 tells us that "a broken spirit dries up the bones." But the first part of that verse offers an antidote: "A joyful heart is good medicine." This Laugh Out Loud section at the end of each chapter is designed to help you **enjoy the lighter side of life**—and leave you smiling.

Heavenly Father, thank you for each mother who has picked up this book. As she holds it in her hands, begin blessing her with the knowledge that You are her best friend and are present to help her. Stir her heart with excitement at what You'll show her on the following pages. Fill her with Your joy, hope, and perspective so she can be the Plan A mom You designed her to be. Help her raise her children not only to be good but also to be godly. In Jesus' name, amen.

WHAT IS A PLAN A WOMAN? WHAT IS A PLAN B WORLD?

Jesus is with us in the Plan B world in which we live,
offering help and hope.

I am with you always, even to the end of the age.

Matthew 28:20

"I'm exhausted. I can't do this." "I must be a horrible mother." "What's wrong with my child? Why can't he/she be like everyone else's?"

I'm convinced that no mother set out to be anything but a good mother. Yet if the truth were known, many of us spent more time preparing the nursery than preparing ourselves to parent a little one. Once our bundle of joy came home from the hospital, who had leisure time to sit and read a book on parenting?

My daughter, Lauren, has a two-year-old son named Logan. She and her husband, Chris, have graciously allowed her father and me to be a part of our grandson's life since before he was born. I sang "Jesus Loves Me" to Lauren's tummy so Logan could hear it in utero. (I told you they were gracious.)

Having Logan has refreshed my early parenting memories. Chris and I laughed on day three of Logan's being home from the hospital when we realized that neither of us had taken a shower. Somehow, in the midst of sitz baths (not ours—we were taking care of Logan while Lauren had hers), grocery shopping, preparing meals, washing, folding clothes, rocking, holding, burping, changing diapers, giving bottles, cheering Lauren through the first days of nursing, and bathing the new little one, we had neglected to take our baths. Can you relate? There are times in parenting when you're so busy and exhausted that you're borderline delirious.

My husband, Keith, and I laugh about one of our delirious moments when Taylor, baby number one, was having a hard night. He couldn't sleep, so neither could we. Keith has always been a great dad and tremendously helpful. That particular night, we took turns getting up with Taylor. Around three a.m. I woke to Taylor's cry, crawled out of bed, and was half way through the family room when Keith and I met, bumping into each other. Startled at running into someone in a pitch-black room, we jumped, gasping, "You scared me!"

"What are you doing?" I blurted, noticing his hands cradled against his chest.

"Walking Taylor," my dear husband whispered, patting his own shoulder.

"Keith!"

With that, he looked down and realized he didn't have Taylor in his arms. He was patting himself as he sleepily paced the floor. Laughing, we went our separate ways—Keith back to bed, me to check on Taylor.

What is a Plan A mom?

The term *Plan A*, at least in this book, is not synonymous with *Type A*, the personality often characterized as impatient, time-conscious, highly competitive, ambitious, business-like, and aggressive.

Rather, a Plan A mom is one who has biblically based desires for herself and her children. She wants to please God and raise her children to know Christ as Savior. She is a mom who prays. She yearns for her children to be healthy, kind to others, and socially and spiritually well adjusted. She tries to make good decisions and wants to raise her children to make good choices.

What is a Plan B world?

Plan B is all that was ushered into the world with the fall of humankind. It's the world in which we live, not the Plan A Garden of Eden that God pronounced good. The Plan B world is the one Jesus described as under Satan's rule (John 12:31; 14:30)—so no doubt, the devil's evil reign affects us, our homes, and our children. We see Satan's influence in violence, pornography, drugs, disrespect, abuse, lies, and more. The Plan B world is filled with sickness, physical disabilities, and threats to our children.

Are there dangers for a Plan A mom in a Plan B world?

Dangers do lurk for a Plan A mom in a Plan B world. Emotionally, moms can become discouraged or feel overwhelmed. Physically, we can become exhausted or even sick. Spiritually, we may feel like giving up or giving in because we think our efforts are to no avail.

A strong-willed child may seem formidable—or a placid child, immovable. An outgoing child may wear you out; a talkative child may wear you down. The mom who has a child with a physical, mental, or emotional disability may not be fighting the evils of the world but may well be fighting her own discouragement, weariness, doubts, and fears.

Plan A moms can forget that it isn't enough for us to go to Bible study. We must be doers of God's Word, not simply hearers. If we want our children to be non-worriers, then we must model prayer. If we want our children to treat others with kindness and respect, then we must model those traits.

As a Plan A mom, you may encounter the "land mines" I mentioned earlier (we'll talk more about these as we journey together through this book)—Plan B mothering practices that stem from what's going on inside your mind and heart. You may struggle with the land mine of control: refusing to give your child to God. The land mine of guilt may keep you chained to your past rather than living in grace. The land mine of discouragement may hobble you, causing you to limp through your days rather than walking with a spring in your step. But for each potential land mine, you can make a choice that leads to blessing. You can disarm those land mines and live in the fullness of God's blessings. You can choose to give your child to God, walk in His grace, and model gratefulness to God and kindness toward others. My goal in this book is to help you learn how to disarm the destructive land mines in your parenting practices and model the Spirit-filled life to your child.

What hope for success is there for a Plan A mom and her children in a Plan B world?

Hope abounds for a Plan A mom and her children in a Plan B world! Why? Because although our feet walk this earth, our spirits have wings to reach heaven. We're not bound by our earthly bodies. God has created a dual means by which we can enjoy our heavenly citizenship while remaining on earth. First, He has sent us a piece of heaven in the form of the Holy Spirit. Because His Spirit dwells within us, we are never alone. Second, God has given us access to His throne room through prayer. We can turn our thoughts heavenward any moment we desire. Living in communion with our Lord is the key to our hope. It's the reason we know we can win the battle against Satan for our children's souls. How do I know? I have seen God's faithfulness as Keith and I raised our son and daughter to know the Lord. I can testify that God is merciful to overlook our shortcomings. He's compassionate and takes up the slack when we give up. He's our friend, who holds our hands and empowers us to parent in a way that honors Him and benefits our children.

Are you exhausted? Are you discouraged by parenting mistakes or worried about traits you see in your child? Keep reading. God sees the mother you can be through His empowerment.

1

A Snoot or a Smile

I defuse the land mine of snootiness and provoking
people by choosing to be kind.

Be kind, one to another.

Ephesians 4:32

Keith and I enjoy babysitting our grandchildren. On one occasion I showed Logan how to form red Play-Doh into lips and a smile. I placed it against my lips and said, "Smile." Logan smiled. Then I showed him the blue Play-Doh. We split it in half and made two big blue eyes. Logan held the blue balls up to his blue eyes and said, "eye." I thought we were doing a great job with our arts-and-crafts/vocabulary lesson when Keith walked in, saw what we were doing, and joined the fun. Except he took the red Play-Doh smile, hung it from his nose, and said "Kachoo!" with a big laugh. I probably don't need to tell you what happened next. Logan took the Play-Doh, put it to his nose, and said, "Kachoo!" Then he cracked up laughing. My eyes widened in horror as I envisioned Logan in preschool acting up with Play-Doh.

If what we taught our children were limited to Play-Doh, everything might be all right. We might simply laugh off what they learn through our example. However, children learn much more than silly antics by watching us. For one thing, they either learn to be kind people, or they learn to be snooty people who provoke others. Unkindness can easily rear its ugly head when plans don't go as we'd like. How can we make sure we're representing Christ's kindness and not letting the rush and stress of life provoke us into acting like rude snoots?

A Contrast of Mothers

If ever there were a contrast between mothers and what they model to their children, it's between Peninnah and Hannah. Although you may be familiar with these two women's stories, their mothering skills deserve a fresh look.

First Samuel 1 takes us to Elkanah's household. When we open the door, we immediately note that he has a problem: two wives. As everyone knows, that's a love triangle that spells disaster. "Elk," as I nicknamed him in *The Plan A Woman in a Plan B World*, goes to church at least once a year. But I'm not sure how meaningful his worship was. Why? First Samuel 1:3 tells us, "The two sons of Eli, Hophni and Phinehas, were priests to the Lord that year." If you know your Bible, that one little verse is full of meaning. Hophni and Phinehas were "worthless men" who did not know the Lord (1 Samuel 2:12).

In addition to the Bible noting the character of the priests, it provides a description of Elk's wives. Hannah is barren and bullied by Peninnah, who is a rude snoot if ever there was one. Although she has many sons and daughters, she views Hannah as a rival and provokes her. Peninnah is not just a snooty woman, she's a snot—an "annoyingly or spitefully unpleasant"[1] person. There's something flowing from her, and it's not the Holy Spirit.

Can you imagine what this woman's children learned from their mother? They learned to be prideful. They learned to be competitive in a negative way. Our competitiveness shouldn't be centered on our bodies or health issues over which we have no control. Our rivals shouldn't be family members.

Not only did Peninnah's children grow up in a home where they were not taught the value of family, they were taught by example how to rudely irritate someone. Twice, the word *provoke* is used in relation to Peninnah. The Hebrew word translated "provoke" in 1 Samuel 1:6 means "to be angry, to provoke to anger."[2] That's how Peninnah treated Hannah. She provoked her to the point of anger.

A Different Mom Model

Think about homes and families with which you're familiar. Do you know someone who won't stop the jabs, snide remarks, criticism, or put-downs? That was Peninnah, and it's characteristic of the carnal human nature. Moms, this is not what we want to model for our children.

In addition to the obvious reasons we don't want to be like Peninnah, there's another. Peninnah's children are never mentioned later in the Bible. Could that be because they adopted her irritating ways of dealing with others and couldn't be used by the Lord? Compare Peninnah and all her children with Hannah, who later bore Samuel, one of the greatest men in the Bible.

As we consider the potential land mines of motherhood in our Plan B world, it's important for us to consider our temperament—our personality and disposition. Are we irritable, like Peninnah, or kind like Hannah? Do we provoke our spouse, children, and others to anger? Or, through prayer and God's enabling, do we treat others with kindness?

Ephesians 6:4 addresses fathers but also is instructional to mothers: "Do not provoke your children to anger, but bring them up in the discipline and instruction of the Lord." This verse emphasizes two points. First, we are not to provoke our children to anger. Second, we are to bring them up in the discipline and instruction of the Lord. The word translated "provoke" in this verse means to "rouse to wrath, exasperate, anger."[3]

Do not provoke your children to anger

How might we provoke our children to anger or exasperation?

Have you ever been in the middle of a project, phone call, or e-mail, and someone demanded your attention that second? There was no warning, such as, "We need to leave the house at 9:45," or "After breakfast could you run this errand for me?" Instead, someone demanded, "In the car. I'm not waiting!" Or, "Stop what you're doing. I need this right now."

Children benefit from being given schedules and having time to prepare for changes in events—just like we do. Consider the following scenarios.

Toddler Amy is intently stacking her blocks, which is both play and work for her. With no warning, Mom walks in, whisks Amy up, lays her on her back to change her diaper and wonders why Amy flails her legs and arms in a screaming fit. Mom gets irritated with her rebellious eighteen-month-old for not cooperatively lying on her back and raises her voice above the wails. "Amy, be still!"

What if, instead, Mom approached her child something like this: "Amy, you're doing so good with your blocks! Now, let's change your wet diaper. Tell your blocks you'll be back. Here, you can hold this one while I change you." I wonder if Mom might not have a better chance of the little one lying still?

Or, consider a ten-year-old boy who is outside riding his bike, getting ready to run a detour course he and his friends have worked hard to erect. Mom pops her head out the front door and says, "Take all that down and get in the car. I need to go to the florist! Hop to it. Now!"

We can hear Johnny's complaint, "Mom, we just set it up. Can't we go in a few minutes?"

"I said, NOW!" Mom demands.

Is Johnny in the above scenario going to gleefully tear down the course he and his friends worked so hard to build? Is he going to happily hop into the car to go to the florist? Or is he going to sulk, which will likely lead to another demand: "Stop sulking right now!"

What might Mom have done to be kinder yet still accomplish her errand? Might she have stuck her head out the door when she saw what they were constructing and warned them, "You boys are working really hard. FYI, though, around ten o'clock, you'll have to take a break, because I need to go to the florist. Why don't you set your course up over there, where it won't be in the way of my car? Then, when we get back, you can pick up where you left off." When the time arrives for her to run her errand, she could say, "Boys, we won't be gone long. Johnny should be back by eleven. Then you can come back and continue your bike course."

As our kids' birthdays roll by, we have countless opportunities to continue positive modeling through our tone of voice, demeanor, and way we treat others either in kindness or rudeness.

A teen who is sarcastic or rude should be corrected immediately. Never should a child be allowed to cuss or speak rudely to another person without Mom correcting the child. Will our kids experiment with ways they hear others speaking? Yes. Even though it may not come from our home, they'll hear various tones and words; or they may erupt from their own temperaments. Still, rudeness should always be addressed. After we address it with them one time, will children immediately be transformed? Not likely. At every stage of life, our children are confronted with their own new set of Plan Bs. Our job and privilege is to help them learn how to appropriately respond in difficult and frustrating times. We do that by modeling kindness, instructing our children, and implementing or allowing appropriate consequences.

Teen Amber walks in and announces she's going to go to a party and spend Friday night with Carly. Mom asks where the party is. Amber replies, "It's none of your business! It's going to be at a friend's house. We're not sure yet."

Mom can either get on Amber's yelling level or be firm but kind. "Amber, you will not talk to me like that. I'm your mother and have every right to ask you questions and to know where you'll be. You can either find out where the party is, and then we'll discuss it, or I can say right now that you're not going. It's your choice. And it won't work for you to spend the night with Carly. We've discussed that before. She's welcome to spend the night at our house, though. Furthermore, I expect an apology for your speaking so rudely to me. I don't speak to you like that, and you're not to speak to me in that tone of voice."

Mom, never "let it go" this "one time." It's never okay for your children to be rude or disrespectful to you.

Kind or exasperating? Kind or demanding? Kind or provoking? Which describes the mother we want to be? Which describes the child you want to have?

Sure, there will be times when moms have to issue unanticipated demands. "Hop in the car. We're out of milk and it's time for the baby to have her bottle. Hurry!" But our tone of voice and explanation play a big part in whether we provoke our children to exasperation or help them understand that life is sometimes interrupted. If it's our routine to be thoughtless of other's schedules and demand they accommodate us at the drop of a hat, we need to consider what we're teaching them. Do we really want our sons to treat their wives that way ("I'm hungry. Let's go.") when perhaps she's in the middle of a phone call? Do we want our daughters to be whiney when others at school don't respond to their demand, "I'm tired of playing ball. Let's go inside." What if playmate Sara is just getting the hang of making baskets and doesn't want to go inside?

Bring them up in the discipline and instruction of the Lord

"Do not provoke your children to anger" is important. However, another directive in Ephesians 6:4 is that we should bring our children up in the discipline and instruction of the Lord. "Bring them up" implies more than a one-time action. We're to continually bring up our children in the discipline and instruction of the Lord, both through our example and through Bible instruction.

There is absolutely no reason for us not to bring up our children in the discipline and instruction or the Lord. Moms, if you have little ones, you have moldable clay. You can raise them to eat sugarcoated cereal, guzzle soft drinks, watch sex and violence on TV, sleep in on Sundays, yell at one another, and use cell phones during meals. Or you can raise them to say, "Good morning. Thank You, God, for this beautiful day"; to bow their heads before meals and thank God for their food. You can bring them up to say, after a meal, "Thank you, Mommy, that was good. May I please be excused?" You can teach politeness by example: "Please close the door." "Please pick up your toys. It's time for bed." "Thank you for helping Mommy." You can teach your children to say, "Yes, Ma'am" and "No, Sir" rather than "Yeah, uh-huh." Children aren't born with a vocabulary and routines. They learn them from us.

If your children are older, and you're thinking, "too late for my kids," that's not true. God meets each of us where we are. If you've been hot-tempered and on the abrupt, rude, loud side, start modeling a kinder spirit—that of Christ. For instance, instead of berating the adulterous woman, Jesus knelt in the sand with her. We can "kneel in the sand" with our children and gracefully direct them to "go and sin no more." If our child went to a party and experimented with alcohol, we might say, "Mark, I know there are tons of temptations for you. I messed up plenty when I was a teenager. But God's desire is for you to live a full life. Getting drunk isn't going to get you there. Laws are in place to protect you and others. You violated God's law to not get drunk. You violated man's laws to not drink at your age. You violated your school's rules. You know you've disappointed Daddy and me. We forgive you, but as a consequence, you'll have to give us the keys to your car. You can have them back when we feel you've regained our trust. Next time you're at a party and someone pulls out alcohol, you can choose to leave and go to a movie. Plan ahead what you'll do. Find a buddy ahead of time to leave with you. You can always use us as an excuse: that we'll take your car away. If your friends say we won't find out, assure them that we will and there will be serious consequences."

Monitor outside influences

In addition to our own behavior and speech influencing how our children treat others, what we permit to come into our home affects our children. Television shows,

DVDs, and computer games should be subject to the "Mom stamp of approval" for appropriate behavior and language.

I remember when *Beavis and Butt-Head* started airing on television. To begin with, I didn't like the name of the show. I didn't want my children calling other children "butt-head." It's even hard for me to type the word because it's crude. Now, mind you, I'm not a prude. I'm not an extremist. However, I felt a God-given responsibility to raise my children in the Lord. That meant drawing the line in the sand. If I didn't allow Taylor and Lauren to call each other butt-head, why would I invite a guest into our home who spoke that way? The same goes for *The Simpsons* and numerous other shows. I just got off the phone with Lauren. In our conversation, I had asked, "Didn't they talk bad in *The Simpsons* too?" She responded with a chuckle, "Mom, I don't know. You didn't let us watch those shows."

Guess what? It's fine with me that she doesn't know. I watched enough to know it wasn't edifying and that I didn't want her and Taylor to talk the way those characters talked. It's not the movie industry's responsibility to decide what's appropriate for our children and grandchildren. It's our responsibility. We can kindly explain to our kids, "I love you and want you to talk nicely to one another. They don't talk nicely in that show, so let's find another one."

Screening entertainment is one thing. What do we do when we have no control over a relative who curses or cuts people down?

In some cases we may find it necessary to limit the amount of time that relative is around our child. Or it may be possible to have a frank discussion with Uncle Bill or Aunt Sally. We should also discuss with our children the differences in speech and behavior—about the fact that we have choices in how we talk to and treat one another. We can explain that God is kind and read Bible verses to them to reinforce our words. We can let them highlight in their own Bible passages such as Ephesians 4:29 and help them to memorize them. We can look for times when they're being kind and compliment them. We might say to four-year-old James, "You're so kind to your baby sister. That makes God happy." We can pray for our children, both in their hearing and in our private prayer time: "Lord, thank You that You are kind and loving. Thank You that James is kind and loving to Amber. Help Amber grow up to be kind and loving."

And we can address times when one isn't kind to the other. To teenage Mark we might say, "It's not okay for you to speak rudely to James. Apologize to him and say what you have to say in a respectful tone."

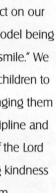

Plan A Mom Tip

What we model has a lasting effect on our children. We model being a snoot or a "smile." We can raise our children to be kind by bringing them up in the discipline and instruction of the Lord and modeling kindness to them.

Sometimes, amid the stress, strain, and competitiveness of life, we may wake up and realize we're more like Peninnah than Hannah. If you're holding to something that causes you to be angry or bitter, I encourage you to diffuse that land mine. You'll find a whole chapter devoted to just that topic in *The Plan A Woman in a Plan B World*.[4] Keep in mind that you're grooming your child to be snooty or to smile by the way you talk to others and to them; by what you allow in the form of books, movies, DVDs, and music; and by whether you consistently remind your children that unwholesome words that tear others down are not to come from their mouths, but rather words that build others up (Ephesians 4:29).

LIVE OUT LOUD

Plan A moms recognize that behavior and attitudes are not just taught, they're "caught." If I make a smile out of Play-Doh, Logan will make a smile. If I make snot, he'll make snot. What are you modeling for your children?

If you recognize that your disposition can be a little on the irritable side or that you're demanding and provoke others rather being kind, begin defusing this land mine. Keep working at it as often as you get a "snoot alert" from the Holy Spirit. To help you evaluate where you are on the snoot-kindness continuum, answer the following questions as honestly as you can.

Plan A Mom Checkup

1. Might "annoyingly or spitefully unpleasant" ever describe you? If so, confess it to the Lord. Tell Him you want to clear that land mine from your mind and life.

2. Ask God to show you what causes you to be irritable. Do you need more sleep? Do you perhaps have a hormone imbalance? Is work stressful? Are you angry because your husband doesn't help or because you feel it's unfair that you're a single mom? Talk to God. Take a journal and pen with you into your prayer time. Write down what He impresses on your heart.

3. Ask God to fill you with His Holy Spirit so that you are a Spirit-filled mom (Galatians 5:22–23), not a Plan B irritable mom (Galatians 5:19–21).

4. Talk to your children and others who have taken the brunt of your unpleasantness. Explain as much or little as you're comfortable with. Apologize.

5. Discuss with your children the difference between living by the Spirit and living by our own fleshly nature. This is the second half of Ephesians 6:4, "bring them up in the discipline and instruction of the Lord." Teach them, "This is Mom's old human nature, but God has given me a new nature by which I can live. I'm going to practice living by God's Spirit, which is kind." This is authentic parenting. This is living out your faith so your children can see that there's a choice what comes out of us: snooty old self or sweet Holy Spirit. Plan A moms practice walking by the Spirit. Mentor your children to walk by the Spirit.

Love Out Loud

1. Read 1 Samuel 1:1–8. Do you recognize any of Peninnah in yourself? Would others say they recognize a touch of Peninnah in you?

2. What do you think Peninnah's children learned from her?

3. How happy do you think Peninnah's home was?

4. Why do you think we don't hear anything more about Peninnah's children?

5. How is God calling you to consider your disposition and how you treat others based on Galatians 5:16–26?

6. Help each other memorize all or part of Ephesians 4:29–32. Share ways you are going to put these verses into practice with your children.

———————— ✦ ————————

BETWEEN YOU AND GOD—PRINCIPLE TO REMEMBER

I defuse the land mine of snootiness
and provoking people to anger by being kind.

Father, Thank You for the reminder that I'm modeling for my children how to treat and speak to others. Help me to wisely monitor what comes into our home and their hearts. Help me to be a positive model. Help me not to provoke my children to anger, but rather to disciple them in Your ways. In Jesus' name, amen.

———————— ✦ ————————

LAUGH OUT LOUD

When Donnie was little, his grandmother tried to teach him to speak correctly. One day Grandma Bunny said, "Donnie, eat your food," to which he replied, "I don't wike it." She immediately corrected him: "I don't like it." Donnie looked up at her with big eyes and said, "You don't wike it either?"—Linda McConnico

Languishing in Guilt
or Rejoicing in Grace

I defuse the land mine of guilt by delighting in the
sweetness and joy of God's grace.

*I acknowledged my sin to You; and my iniquity I did not hide; I said, 'I will
confess my transgressions to the Lord'; and You forgave the guilt of my sin.*

Psalm 32:5

"I feel so bad. I didn't know Christ when my children were little. I didn't raise
them to know the Lord."

"I must be the most terrible mother in the world. When I think back to the times
I lost my temper, spanked them too hard. . . . "

"I thought I was doing the right thing by never telling my kids, no. Now they're
self-absorbed, self-indulgent adults."

"I feel horrible. I was a struggling single mom and was thrilled for my kids to
watch TV so I could fix dinner or pay the bills. They grew up watching violence and
sex and hearing disrespectful language. One son is in jail. My daughter got pregnant
out of wedlock and is married to a man who treats her disrespectfully."

"My daughter called last week from college and told me she's a lesbian. I grew up
in a very tolerant church, so I never explained to my children we all have tendencies

to sin but that it doesn't mean it's okay to act on our impulses—whether they be genetic, sensual, emotional, or to lie or steal."

Do you have regrets as a mom? Maybe they're not as dramatic as some of these examples—or maybe they're more so. Every mother knows what it's like to feel guilt over some parenting flaw—but God doesn't want us to live with guilt. He wants us to experience His grace and model it to our children.

Innocence Lost

If ever a mother felt qualified to wear a scarlet *G*, for guilt, around her neck, it would be Eve. I don't know the cause of your guilty feelings, but none of us could compete with her in the reason-for-remorse arena: "I'm the one who introduced sin into the world. As a result, we were cast from Eden. My son Cain killed my son Abel."

Eve took hold of the forbidden, put it to her lips, and bit into Satan's lie. What were the consequences of her not believing God and listening to the devil?

At first, for a pleasurable moment, it seemed there were no consequences. So she engaged Adam in her sin as well. And then it happened. The eyes of both of them were opened, and they knew that they were naked (Genesis 3:7).

Having swallowed their sin, they put themselves in the chokehold of its consequences:

- Innocence lost
- Hiding
- Fear
- Blame
- Enmity
- Multiplied pain in childbirth
- Altered marriage relationship
- Cursed ground full of thorns and thistles
- Sweat-producing, backbreaking work
- Physical death—return to dust
- Death of sacrificial animal
- Knowledge of good and evil
- Banned from the Garden of Eden
- Cultivating the ground from which they were taken

- Spiritual death
- Anger
- One son murdered by another son
- Wandering
- Separated from God

This couple's fleeting moments of pleasure, when they swallowed Satan's lie and rebelled against God's truth, resulted in the death of their purity and the end of their glorious walk with God.

Yet even amid the flood of consequences, God provided a way for the guilt, the perversity of their sin, to be removed from their backs. He made a covering of animal skin. His provision cost an animal its life. Its blood was spilled so Adam and Eve wouldn't be reminded daily of their nakedness. The animal's sacrificial death foreshadowed Christ's sacrificial death, which would one day pay for the sins of all people. Anyone and everyone is invited to God through this sacrificial atonement and covering.

Yes, Eve swallowed the poison of sin when she tasted the forbidden. However, God provided the antidote in another swallow: "Death is swallowed up in victory" (1 Corinthians 15:54). Who accomplished the great feat of swallowing death so we might have eternal life? Christ.

Guilt Defined

When we speak of the guilt we have in relation to parenting, or perhaps the guilt our children live with, it's important to understand the true definition of guilt and the distinction between guilt and its afterglow of guilt, shame.

In the Bible, two Hebrew words are primarily used for *guilt*. One is ¢*ashmah*, which means "offense, sin, wrongdoing."[1] Ezra uses this word when he says, "O my God, I am ashamed and embarrassed to lift up my face to You, my God, for our iniquities have risen above our heads and our guilt has grown even to the heavens" (Ezra 9:6). Ezra says our wrongdoings have piled up.

The second word for *guilt* is ¢*avon*, which means "perversity, depravity, iniquity, consequence of or punishment for iniquity."[2] King David used this word in relation to his guilt: "I acknowledged my sin to You; and my iniquity I did not hide; I said, 'I will confess my transgressions to the Lord' and You forgave the guilt of my sin." God forgave the perversity and depravity of David's sin.

Eternal Guilt versus Daily Guilt

The Bible teaches that all have sinned and that there are two kinds of guilt: eternal guilt and daily guilt. Eternal guilt has to do with our general sinful human condition—that we need salvation from the guilt of that sinfulness. The Bible warns that if we don't admit we're sinners, repent, and come to Him through Christ's blood, which atones for our sin, then we won't be able to be with Him in heaven. Rather, we'll die in our sins (John 8:24) and be judged (Revelation 20:13).

Plan A Mom Tip

Teach your children to sincerely confess their sins to God.

Once we repent of our sin and are forgiven, sealed with the Holy Spirit, and set apart for God, we're to keep being cleansed of our daily guilt through confession. We're not to continue in sin but rather to learn God's ways and, through the empowerment of the Holy Spirit, walk in them. We will, of course, like toddlers, stumble and fall, which is why daily confession is critical (1 John 1:9).

Genuine Guilt versus False Guilt

Sin and guilt are linked. If we're committing adultery, we're bound in our sin and guilt, liable to God, and worthy of punishment. We feel guilty (unless we've hardened our hearts against the Holy Spirit, who convicts us of our sin) because we are genuinely guilty.

If we repent and confess our sin to God, He forgives the guilt (perversity, depravity) of our sin. We're cleansed (1 John 1:9).

False guilt, on the other hand, is based on self-condemning feelings that we haven't lived up to our own expectations or those of someone else. As a friend of mine, Deana Mattingly Blackburn points out, "It can be problematic to think automatically that guilt is from God; conviction by the Holy Spirit is from God. Guilt is strongly influenced by culture. (Hence, peer pressure.) Discernment is crucial (James 1:5). Hold the guilt-producing decision/action up to God's Word as the measure, not cultural influences. Guilt can too easily become a habit."

For purposes of this chapter, we're dealing with genuine guilt.

Why Guilt Lingers

In truth, once we repent and are cleansed of our sin, our guilt doesn't linger. What lingers is Satan, our accuser (Revelation 12:10). He taunts us. He doesn't want us to rejoice and live in the beauty, sweetness, loveliness, charm, and joy of God's grace. If we aren't careful, we'll live like the child who broke his mother's remote and is forgiven but continues to cry and hang his head in shame, not accepting or enjoying her love.

The word *guilt* is found ninety-five times in the Bible. But only six of those instances are in the New Testament, and then only in reference Christ and there being no guilt in Him. *Guilty* is used forty-four times, but only four of those are in the New Testament. It means "bound, under obligation, liable, worthy of punishment."[3]

The Greek word for *grace*, which is what God extends and we experience both for eternity and in our cleansed daily walk, is *charis*. It means "that which affords joy, pleasure, delight, sweetness, charm, loveliness, good will, loving-kindness, favor; of the merciful kindness by which God, exerting his holy influence upon souls, turns them to Christ, keeps, strengthens, increases them in Christian faith, knowledge, affection, and kindles them to the exercise of the Christian virtues."[4]

The New Testament is filled with verses affirming Jesus' grace, His sweetness, charm, loveliness, good will, and favor toward us. "For of His fullness we have all received, and grace upon grace" (John 1:16).

Following, a dear mom shares how she chooses to live in God's grace rather than let guilt get the better of her.

> I became very familiar with the area of town where my daughter was living on the streets. Bars, clubs, adult theatres, the Night Shelter. One afternoon, while I was driving around looking for Mindy, I caught a glimpse of her going into an old, abandoned house. I was grateful. The old house seemed safer to me than when she was just out on the streets. I'll never forget that day. Driving up, getting out of my car, walking thru the weeds, and looking through a window to seeing her, sitting cross-legged on a bare, dirty floor—with her open Bible in her lap. The tough, hard shell that I had wrapped around my heart broke open that day. I cried until I was completely exhausted. How could this be real? How could she have fallen so deep into

the world of drugs? I couldn't reach her. Not only could she not hear my voice, but she refused my touch—my love. Her only desire was for more heroin and cocaine. As I write this, thirty-two years later, the indescribable pain I in my heart is as real as it was the day I stood there staring at my beautiful, drug-addicted daughter.

The old house became the first place I would look. If I could just see her, I would know she was alive. At night I'd hide behind a huge dumpster across the street from the Night Shelter. The "street people" would line up to get inside so they would have a bed for the night. When the beds were full, the others were sent away. Oh, how I would pray she would get in. Especially in the winter. If she made it inside, I would feel relief . . . and then my thoughts would turn to what could happen to her during the night. If she didn't get in, no matter how hard I begged, she wouldn't come home with me. She had chosen another world.

My prayer during those times was always the same. Please, God . . . please protect her. I know You love her. I know You're sovereign. She's suffering the consequences for my screwed-up life. Let me suffer the consequences of my bad choices . . . marrying without considering You . . . finding myself an abused, divorced woman with three children. There was no question in my mind: the choices Mindy was making were my fault. I never blamed God or anyone else. Only myself. I was her mother. It had to be my fault.

Sometime during these days of searching, finding her, not finding her, begging her to come home, crying myself to sleep, I slowly began to surrender her to the Lord. I had done everything I knew to do. She had been in several treatment centers and would go right back to using as soon as she was released. I had even sought professional advice for my own behavior.

It didn't happen suddenly, but as I searched the Scriptures, I slowly began to accept God's grace. I knew my sins, my mistakes, my choices, whatever one wishes to call being out of God's will, were forgiven. I had fallen on my face many times thanking Him for His forgiveness. But somehow I couldn't forgive myself. Nor could I release the guilt I felt for my daughter's unhappiness. I began to understand that God's grace is always undeserved. I began to understand that the shame and guilt I was holding on to was breaking His heart, just as Mindy's behavior was breaking mine. As I embraced more and more of His love and grace, I released more and more of my guilt and shame. I began to claim Scriptures. I learned to thank God for *who He is. To be grateful for His unconditional love for me and my daughter. I can now feel responsibility without feeling guilt. Satan still comes at me with thoughts and feelings of guilt, but praise God, I have learned to stand against him.*

Mindy no longer uses drugs. For that I am so thankful. But her mind is damaged from the years of cocaine and heroin. Her life isn't what this Plan A mom dreamed it would be. But she loves the Lord, and after many years of discord, she again loves me.

I share these painful memories in the hope that you'll realize much more quickly than I did to "choose grace"! I pray God will comfort you as He has comforted me.

Grace Tips from a Plan A Mom in a Plan B World

If you've confessed that which is clearly explained in God's Word as sin against Him, and He's removed your guilt, be proactive. Walk in God's grace. Model it to your children.

1. Study the topic of grace. "Grace" is used 131 times in the Bible, 121 of those times in the New Testament. Learn about God's gift to you.

2. Slowly meditate on each of the following definitions of grace: that which affords joy, pleasure, delight, sweetness, charm, loveliness, good will, loving-kindness, favor; of the merciful kindness by which God, exerting His holy influence upon souls, turns them to Christ, keeps, strengthens, increases them in Christian faith, knowledge, affection, and kindles them to the exercise of the Christian virtues.[5]

3. Do as Hebrews 4:16 instructs: draw near with confidence to the throne of grace, so you may receive mercy and find grace to help in time of need.

4. Make it your mission to grow in the grace and knowledge of your Lord and Savior Jesus Christ (2 Peter 3:18).

5. Use God's Word to stand against Satan's accusations. When the accuser brings up sins that you've already confessed and tries to reinstall the guilt God has removed, take a stand (Ephesians 6:14) as Christ did, with the truth of Scripture. Memorize and take to heart 1 John 1:9.

6. Speak the following, as they apply (or draft your own) to Satan as
   often as necessary!
   - "Yes, I committed adultery. No, I'm not an adulterer any more.
     Jesus has cleansed me and forgiven the guilt of my sin. Be gone!"
   - "Yes, I failed to bring my children up in the disciplines and
     instructions of the Lord. No, God doesn't continue to hold me
     guilty. God has forgiven me. Be gone!"
   - "Yes, I provoked my children to wrath. No, I didn't walk by the
     Spirit as commanded. But my children aren't bound by my sin.
     God can redeem them as He has me. Nothing is impossible with
     Him. Be gone!"
7. Refuse to entertain wrong feelings. Emotions are a gift of the
   Lord, but they can be used as a tool of Satan. Carefully guard your
   emotions. Check them against God's Word (start with Galatians
   5:22–23). Learn to distinguish between godly sorrow that leads
   you to repentance (John 16:8; 2 Corinthians 7:10) and Satan's
   emotionally draining accusations (Revelation 12:10).

Modeling God's Grace for Your Children

In our Plan B worlds, we moms are going to sin. We're going to do things, say things, and act in ways that make us want to hang our head in shame until we go to our grave. But God doesn't want us to go to our graves in guilt. He extended His favor to us even when we were sinners and didn't deserve it. That's the whole marvelous, incomprehensible thing about grace. We're so used to being performance driven that it's hard for us to grasp God's loving us and forgiving us just because He loves us and wants to forgive us. But that is the message of salvation.

Our children are going to mess up royally . . . perhaps day after day after day. Just when you finally get through one stage with your kids and think you're over the hump, you'll turn around and find you're already in the next stage, with a whole new set of skills to teach them.

How can you best prepare your children for their relationship with the Lord? Teach them respect for your authority so they will one day have respect for God's authority. Teach them who God is, His attributes and character. Hold them accountable for their behavior. Let them suffer the consequences of their actions. Exercise loving but swift discipline rather than holding things over their heads. Be quick to forgive when they repent and tell you they're sorry. Model God's grace and love—let them live in the same delight, joy, and sweetness God extends to you.

Live Out Loud

Plan A Mom Checkup

Use the following to begin disarming the land mine of guilt. Stop languishing and start rejoicing in God's grace.

1. Do I live in the joy and sweetness of God's grace, or am I languishing in guilt?
2. When faced with a Plan B situation or child, do I listen to Satan's accusations or use truth and Scripture to stand against him?
3. If you've never repented of your sin and received Christ as Savior, you can pray this prayer. "Dear God, I know I'm a sinner. I have failed You, my children, and others. Please forgive me. I desire to know You as Lord and Savior and to stop walking in my sinful ways. Please cleanse me and fill me with Your Holy Spirit. I love You and thank You. In Jesus' name, amen."
4. Share with your children and others that you've asked for God's forgiveness and received His grace. Apologize to your kids for your shortcomings, and ask them to forgive you for any wrongs you've done against them.
5. Begin each day by praising God for forgiving you and rejoicing in His grace. Be quick to repent of daily sin.
6. Teach your children the difference between false and genuine guilt.
7. Pray for your children to be sensitive to the conviction of the Holy Spirit. Be sensitive to when they want to repent of their sin and accept Jesus as their Savior. Lead your children to say prayers of repentance when they willfully disobey you. Include thanksgiving to God for His forgiveness. Teach them that God removes guilt and train them in how to use Scripture to stand against lingering feelings of guilt.

LOVE OUT LOUD

1. Why do you think we're often prone to languish in guilt rather than rejoice in grace?

2. Revelation 12:10 describes Satan as the accuser of the brethren. Why do you think Satan likes to accuse us? What benefit is it to him?

3. In what way are you encouraged by Psalm 103:12–14?

4. What difference does Psalm 35:2 make to you—knowing God has forgiven the guilt of your sin?

5. What benefit to God is it when you walk in the joy of His grace rather than languishing in guilt? Read 2 Timothy 2:20–22.

6. How does Ephesians 2:8–10 tie in with 2 Timothy 2:20–22?

7.. What did you gain from the testimony of the mom in this chapter about how she's moved from guilt to grace?

8. Share scriptures you use to stand against Satan's accusations.

BETWEEN YOU AND GOD—PRINCIPLE TO REMEMBER

I defuse the land mine of guilt by
delighting in the sweetness and joy of God's grace.

Father, thank You for the sweetness, delight, and joy of grace. Thank You for removing the guilt of my sin. I love You and praise You! Help me not to hold things over my children's heads but to extend grace to them as You've extended it to me. In Jesus' name, Amen.

LAUGH OUT LOUD

When Sean was almost four, he was entertaining himself so well in his room that I, his naive and unsuspecting mom, decided to enjoy a cup of tea and a few pages of the novel of the month. I say novel of the *month* because as any mother of two preschoolers knows there are about thirty seconds in each day when you can actually put together enough brain cells to understand anything written above a three-year-old comprehension level.

Anyway, things had been perhaps a little too quiet, so when Sean came into the kitchen beaming with pride and led me to his room, I have to admit feeling a little fear and trepidation. When we reached the threshold of his sanctuary, my precious little artist threw his hands in the air and said, "Look Mommy!" He had used a screw to etch his name into the headboard of his bunk.

What could I say? He was filled with innocent joy at his masterpiece. While some might see what Sean had done as defacing a piece of furniture, to me it was his four-year-old way of trying to please his mom.

Don't you know God must get a good laugh out of our peculiar attempts to please Him? Aren't you grateful that He knows exactly where we are in our spiritual growth process?—Kellie Kendrick

3

I HAVE TO or I GET TO

I defuse the land mine of drudgery by
developing an attitude of gratitude.

*Let the peace of Christ rule in your hearts, to which indeed
you were called in one body; and be thankful.*

Colossians 3:15

"Live like today was your last day on earth." I have no idea who came up with that saying, but no doubt he or she was an optimist. I wonder if it was a woman whose day consisted of dragging herself out of bed to the sound of a crying infant; diapering and dressing toddlers; and prodding elementary-age kids to find their backpacks, eat, and catch the school bus while arguing with her tween, who wants to dress like a pop star—all as the cat jumps onto the kitchen counter, spilling the cereal, and the dog chews on her new shoe.

We may ask, if this were my last day on earth, what would I do differently? On one hand, we might want to bop the person who cheers us to live like it's our last day. On the other hand, we might truly benefit from pausing and taking inventory: what *would* I do differently if today were my last day on earth?

Do has always been the word that trips me in that piece of introspection. Often, in books and movies like *The Bucket List*, when characters are told they only have a short time to live, they jet around the world doing all the things they've wanted to do. However, to me, the key word in living well is *be*. Even if this were my last day on earth, if I'm the mom in the first paragraph, I'm not going to jet around the world. I'm going to do the same things I'm doing, because that's my life. And I don't know it's my last day. The challenge really is more a question of attitude.

What about you? How often do you wake up and dread your day? A mom who is a nurse's aide may wake, thinking she can't take one more day of cleaning up after patients only to come home and clean up after her kids. A mom who's a cook may plod to work not knowing how many more potatoes she can peel there and then return home to cook a meal for her family. A mom who's a psychiatrist may not know how many more troubled people she can listen to when she's dealing with her own troubled teen. A mom may not know how much more of her husband's anger she can stand as she drudges through her day worrying her son will become like his father. Even a happy mom may think to herself, "I don't know how many more diapers and crib sheets I can change today!"

Drudgery can be a land mine. It can lie subtly beneath the surface of our nicely clad bodies. It can lie buried in the recesses of our hearts. As routines become monotonous and fatiguing, we can be left uninspired and joyless.

Lauren Spalding, my daughter, shares how she chose an attitude of gratitude and the difference it made in her Plan B day and in her son's day:

Being a mother is the most incredible blessing God has ever bestowed on me. I'm so thankful to be a mom, but that definitely isn't always in the forefront of my mind. I have a beautiful, bouncy, busy, toddler who is as strong-willed as I am! People often ask me if I am exhausted at the end of the day. Of course I am! Sometimes it's easy to fall into a pit of exhaustion and have a negative attitude. "I really wish he'd sit and play quietly instead of constantly climbing on the table or couch or stairs and wanting to go outside in the hundred-degree heat. I wish he would nap longer, like Johnny."

For instance, earlier this week my son woke from his nap much earlier than usual. I was in the middle of working from home and had much to do. At first, my fleshly thoughts were, "You've got to be kidding me! How is he already up? What am I going to do for the rest of the day?" But I quickly decided to have a positive attitude instead of a negative one (although I admit I don't always). Because of my attitude change, when I went upstairs, I was excited, so excited, to see my son. We had some of the most precious moments. I held him in my lap, facing me, and we had some quiet playtime. I showed him how to smile on demand, and he had such a cute expression in his eyes. We tickled, gave hugs, loved on each other, and it was a truly memorable and sweet time. Had I not purposefully chosen to change my attitude, it would have been so easy to just get him from his crib, get him a drink and snack and think, "Poor me." Think what I would have missed!

I'm thankful to have a happy, healthy son. I'm thankful for the precious moments in life that might sometimes be taken for granted.

In Proverbs 22:6 God calls us to "train up a child in the way he should go; even when he is old he will not depart from it." Deuteronomy 6:7 says, "You shall teach them [God's laws] diligently to your children, and shall talk of them when you sit in your house, and when you walk by the way, and when you lie down, and when you rise." If we train our children, by our example, to have a negative attitude and not to be grateful and appreciative, they'll grow up that way. We need to model a positive attitude for our kids. It's so important to teach them the road to God by example; by the way we talk and act. I hope there will be many more times when my son sees me set an example of gratitude.

One Word That Can Change Your Life

I know. You're not easily buying that one word can change your life. But it can.

Think with me for a minute. Jesus said the things that come out of our mouths come from the heart (Matthew 15:18). Since what's in our hearts spills out of our mouths, and our heartfelt thoughts and words materialize into actions, it's worthwhile to consider what's in our hearts. Is it "I have to" or "I get to"?

We need to remove from our hearts the land mine of drudgery—"I *have* to"—and replace it with "I *get* to." Try it on for size. How would you fill in the blank? "I have to_____." Now, using the same word, change "have to" to "get to": "I get to_____." By replacing "have" with "get," you defuse a land mine of negativity. You choose a perspective that propels you from drudgery to living in the optimism of your God-given day. I speak from experience. Many times I have thought, "I have to . . . " Then God reminds me that it's a privilege to fulfill that which He's given me to do; and remembering that changes my attitude from "have to" to "get to."

How might it play out for you in your Plan B moments, when your child comes in past curfew or baby wakes at four instead of six a.m.? What's a typical first thought? "Oh, no." Second thought: "I'm so tired." Third thought: "I'm exhausted." Fourth thought: "I wish I could roll over and go back to sleep." Fifth thought: "I have to get up." Now, replace that fifth thought with, "I get to get up. I'm alive. My legs work. My feet work. God has prepared me for this moment, this day, to take care of this child, to listen to this teen, to train this toddler so he or she will grow to know and serve the Lord."

Try it. I challenge you to switch from "have to" to "get to." When you make it a practice, you'll discover you have more than a word switch. You'll also see a change in your attitude, from drudgery to hope-filled purpose—an attitude that is as contagious with your children as Lauren's smile was with Logan.

A "Get To" Mom and Great-Grandmother

One person I believe exemplifies a "get to" attitude in her Plan B world is Ruth, the biblical King David's great-grandmother.

Since many of you are already familiar with Ruth's story, I'll only summarize it here. Her husband had died, so she returned with her widowed mother-in-law, Naomi, to Naomi's hometown, Bethlehem. There Ruth worked in the grain fields, salvaging what the employed reapers left behind for the poor. In keeping with the custom of the day, Naomi sent Ruth to a distant relative to see if he would take her as his wife, thus securing their future. Boaz did marry Ruth, and they had a child named Obed.

My, my. If Ruth were to read my five-sentence synopsis of her life, she would certainly call out from heaven, "But it wasn't that simple!"

For Ruth's sake, let's look more closely at her Plan B . . . at her tearstained pillow. Let's look deep within her heart as she wondered how she could make it without a husband. Let's wonder what went on in her pretty little head as Naomi complained, "woe is me," day after day. Let's watch Ruth rub her sore feet after traveling from Moab to Bethlehem. Let's take Ruth's hands in ours, turn them over, and put ointment on her blisters after a long day in the fields. Let's rub her back, sore from stooping all day in the fields. Let's watch the black-cloaked Ruth, in the middle of the night, secretly approach the sleeping Boaz and lie down at his feet. Let's watch her fingers, trembling, slowly reach to uncover his feet to wake him. Let's look deep into Ruth's dark eyes as she waited for a reaction from the man who would either agree to care for her or reject her.

There, we're a little closer to real life.

But what if we could ask, "Ruth, what made you tick? How did you put up with Naomi's whining when your husband had died too; when you were doing all the work? How did you carry out the "lay at Boaz's feet" ordeal and marry a man you hardly knew, who was much older than you? Did you feel you had no choice?

If we could hear Ruth's reply, I think it would be, "Yes, I felt I had to. But I also felt that I *got* to. I felt God calling me to be a support to Naomi. I felt grateful to know her God. I was thankful that I got to work in a safe field, where grain was intentionally left for me. I felt blessed because Boaz was a good man and was willing to take me as his wife and provide for me and my mother-in-law. I was thankful that I got to bear a child and bless Naomi with a grandson. I *got to* become David's great-grandmother!"

Why do I believe Ruth is a model of a "get to" woman and mom in a Plan B world (besides the fact that God honored her by naming a book of the Bible after her)? Watch her. Listen to her. Contrast her with Naomi, who bemoaned her lot in life and attributed her circumstances to, "the Lord's hand has gone forth against me" (Ruth 1:13).

In Ruth 1:14 we see Ruth's first "get to" choice. She didn't have to say to Naomi, "Where you go, I will go. Your people shall be my people, and your God, my God" (Ruth 1:16). Her outlook was one of optimism: "I get to." Her attitude was one of commitment: "Where you die, I will die" (Ruth 1:17). Ruth was "determined," according to Ruth 1:18.

The Hebrew word here translated "determined" means "to be strong, alert, courageous, brave, stout, bold, solid, hard; to strengthen, persist.[1]

Friends, we can choose to be determined, "get to" moms. Instead of feeling sorry for ourselves and trudging through our lives, we can ask God to make us strong, alert, courageous, brave, bold, and solid. We can ask Him to strengthen us with the Holy Spirit and help us persist with a "get to" attitude and with the mind of Christ. We can recognize that "have to" are words Satan can infuse with self-pity, self-absorption, and drudgery. "Get to" are words God can infuse with His perspective and that can influence our children to adopt an attitude of gratitude.

A Command, Not a Suggestion

Christian motivational speaker Zig Ziglar has said, "The healthiest of all emotions is gratitude."[2] Is that why God does more than *urge* us to be grateful? He *commands* us to be thankful: "Let the peace of Christ rule in your hearts, to which indeed you were called in one body; and be thankful" (Colossians 3:15).

In this verse, the Greek word for "thankful" means "mindful of favours, grateful."[3] The verb tense is a command, and not just a command to be thankful one time. Dr. Gleason Archer explains the verb tense as a "commitment to a long term way of doing something. A command to keep on doing an action as one's general habit or life-style. Repeat each time this situation arises!"[4]

Plan A Mom Tip

Defuse the land mine of drudgery. Adopt an attitude of gratitude. Model it to your children.

Moms, we can develop an attitude of gratitude.

Attitude is defined as a mental position with regard to a fact or state, a feeling or emotion toward a fact or state.[5] *Gratitude* is defined as the state of being grateful: thankfulness.[6] Which "tude" best describes you: atti or grati? Have to or get to? Are you known as having an attitude or being filled with gratitude?

Live Out Loud

Plan A Mom Checkup

Use the following to help you disarm drudgery, develop an attitude of gratitude, and influence your children to have an attitude of gratitude.

1. When faced with a Plan B situation, child, or responsibility, is my attitude one of drudgery or gratitude?
2. If my child grows up to be like me, will he or she be characterized as having an "attitude" or gratitude?

3. Am I willing to confess that I've ignored God's command to be thankful as part of my general habit and lifestyle? (If so, repent. Prayerfully commit to a long-term way of being thankful. Anytime a "have to" thought arises, switch the "have" to a "get.")

4. Each morning, focus on one of God's attributes for which you are thankful. For instance, one attribute is that He is our "Abba Father." Let that thought rule your mind all day. When Plan B moments hit, turn to your Abba Father. The next day, select another of God's attributes for which to be thankful. In your prayer time, build on that for which you are thankful. Invite your children to chime in. You might begin, "Heavenly Father, thank You for being our Abba Father." On day two, Johnny can add, "Thank You that You abide forever." On day three, add another of God's attributes for which you're thankful. At the end of the year, even if Plan B has pulled the rug out from under you, you and your children will have 365 reasons to be thankful. A sample of *365 A–Z Names, Titles, and Attributes of God*[7] can be found in the appendix at the end of this book.

5. Memorize Colossians 3:15. Help your children memorize it.

6. Adopt a lifestyle of gratitude.

Love Out Loud

1. Which comes most naturally, an "attitude" or gratitude?

2. What did you learn from Ruth about gratitude?

3. Discuss the definitions of *attitude* and *gratitude* and the verb tense of "be thankful."

4. Find additional verses in the Bible that command you to be thankful. Why is it important for you to model an attitude of gratitude and thankfulness to your children?

5. Discuss the benefits of teaching your children to center their thankfulness on God and who He is.

6. For which of the attributes listed in the appendix are you most thankful? Why?

Between You and God—Principle to Remember

I defuse the land mine of drudgery by living with an attitude of gratitude.

Father, help me practice a "get to" rather than a "have to" attitude—one that honors You and models a thankful spirit to my children. Help them develop a thankful attitude, one filled with gratitude for You. In Jesus' name, amen.

Laugh Out Loud

When our children were babies, their pediatrician wrote out a prescription for their daddy:

Name: Keith Williams
RX: Ear muffs. 1 pair, extra large. Wear nightly.

4

My Way or God's Way

I defuse the land mine of manipulation by
doing things God's way.

Commit your way to the Lord, trust also in Him, and He will do it.

Psalm 37:5

Sitting in the courtroom, I stared at the man robed in black and prayed for his wisdom. Carol and Mark, divorced parents, sat at opposing counsels' tables and stared at Keith, each hoping my husband would rule in their favor. Bryan, their son, fretted in an adjoining room, hoping Keith would rule that he could live with his father.

Watching this family drama, I couldn't help but hurt for all involved. A range of emotions from love to anger racked each home. However, emotion was not the only factor in play. Manipulation set the stage for the day's events. Bryan's father promised him a car if he went to live with him. The mother, who had raised him, couldn't compete with this bribe. She'd resorted to tears and threatening Bryan that if he lived with his dad, she couldn't go on.

Any divorced parent will tell you that manipulation is a land mine. While it's often apparent in divorce situations, it's present in lots of married family homes too. Consider the following daughter's comment about her mother.

My mother has been a manipulative, self-centered person for as long as I can remember. I was brought up to feel guilty about everything. I have one brother, and neither of us wants anything to do with her. Recently she was in the hospital, and although we tried to be there as much as possible, she accused us of not paying attention to her. Today I just about lost it. She called and asked if I could take her to her follow-up appointment. All I said was, could she check with my brother. I had already taken off a lot of time from work, and I was hoping he could take her. Her response? She hung up on me. I called her back and asked her why. She said, "Because I can tell I'm too much trouble for you." My stomach literally gets tied up in knots when I see her number on my caller ID.

After reading the above, I stared at my computer screen and prayed I wasn't a manipulative mother. I racked my brain for thoughtless words I'd said to Taylor and Lauren in their younger years. Then I thought, "What about now that they're married? What about with their precious spouses? Do I come across as trying to get my way and make them feel bad if I don't?" I've already made up my mind to call and ask those very questions. If so, an apology will be offered and quickly followed by a determined effort to rectify my behavior.

Is manipulation always verbal? Hardly. Think about the kind of relational skills we teach our children when we stomp out of a room, roll our eyes, give someone the silent treatment, or slam the door when we don't get our way. Of course there's also the verbal manipulation we use to attempt to guilt someone into doing what we want.

Manipulation—A Learned Skill

What is manipulation? The dictionary tells us it's "to control or play upon by artful, unfair, or insidious means especially to one's own advantage, to change by artful or unfair means so as to serve one's purpose."[1] My friends have offered a variety of their own insights on manipulation:

"I wouldn't know how to get Jack to do anything if I didn't manipulate him."

"I don't know when I start and stop manipulating. I've done it for so long."

"I think we're born manipulators."

"Moms spend the first eight years of their children's lives manipulating them."

I had to chuckle at the last comment. "True," I had to admit. However, to control by artful means to serve our own purposes when trying to get a toddler to eat breakfast isn't quite a parenting land mine. I doubt there's a mom who hasn't coaxed her little one, "We'll play outside after you eat your breakfast."

No, the Plan A mom concern we're addressing is more insidious. This manipulation is to control or play upon by artful, unfair means to one's own advantage. And nowhere in the Bible do we have a better example of a manipulative mother than Rebekah.

If we take a close look at Rebekah and her brother, Laban, we find a common characteristic: both are skilled manipulators. Rebekah schemes for Isaac to bless Jacob rather than Esau. Laban schemes for Jacob to marry Leah rather than Rachel. From whom did they learn to manipulate? Was it from their mother, the same way Jacob learned from Rebekah? Although we don't know, it causes us to wonder. Relational skills are caught as much as taught. Life is a classroom. We moms are the teachers, our children the students. They learn how to treat people, solve problems, work out differences, and accomplish the ends they desire by watching us.

Genesis 24 introduces us to Rebekah. Her marriage to Isaac is one of the greatest love stories in the Bible. However, Rebekah, like Sarah, her mother-in-law, was barren for years. Isaac, unlike men often did in those days, didn't take a second wife to bear his child. Rather, he prayed for her (Genesis 25:21). He waited on God to answer his prayers and for Rebekah to conceive, which she eventually did.

Plan A Mom Tip

When you don't understand what's going on with your child, instead of reacting or ignoring the concern, inquire of the Lord and listen to His reply.

Rebekah also had a prayer life—or at least she developed one when her womb became a war zone. Genesis 25:22 tells us, "the children struggled together within her, and she said, 'If it is so, why then, am I this way?' So she went to inquire of the Lord."

I love that! Rebekah didn't have access to a sonogram, so she asked God what was happening within her. Not only did she inquire, but she also listened to God's explanation: she had two future nations (twins) within her. The older would serve the younger, a reversal of what ancient culture considered the natural order.

Plan B Twins

Isaac and Rebekah were married for twenty years when Jacob and Esau were born. It would be nice to think things were blissful after the twins' birth; but we know that, while children are a gift from the Lord, they also make life more complicated. No couple is immune to parenting's trials and tension, including Rebekah and Isaac. Each had their favorite son. Isaac loved Esau because he had a taste for game, but Rebekah loved Jacob (Genesis 25:27–28). Can you envision this couple's Plan B household, with each parent favoring a different sibling?

Plan A Mom Tip

Perhaps you're nodding and thinking, "This describes my kids. They're opposites!" What can we learn from the way Isaac and Rebekah parented? First, guard against favoritism. Second, look more than skin deep. Observe the inner person of your child's heart. Furthermore, in light of our topic for this chapter, we learn the danger of manipulation and importance of not passing this relational skill to our children.

Jacob is described as a peaceful man, living in tents. The Hebrew word translated "peaceful" in this verse means "perfect, complete, one who lacks nothing in physical strength, beauty; sound, wholesome, an ordinary, quiet sort of person; morally innocent, having integrity."[2] It's the same word used to describe Job when the Bible says he was blameless (Job 1:8). "Living in tents" identifies his occupation: caring for the flocks and herds.

Esau was into hunting, although the family had no need for venison—they had flocks and herds. Maybe Isaac enjoyed the change in menu. Yet what a sad commentary on the reason Isaac loved this child more. Esau had no interest in God's covenant promises. Hebrews 12:16 uses two words to describe Esau: immoral and godless.

Planning versus Manipulation

What's the difference between manipulation and simple planning? Is it a sin to take proactive steps to acquire what we want? It could be, if we're planned something we know is against God's will. However, to have a goal in accordance with God's will and take steps to attain it isn't a sin. Genesis 25:29–34 provides such a case.

A Plan in Accordance with God's Will

Although we're not given details, it's reasonable to assume that Rebekah told Jacob of the prophecy that his older brother would one day serve him. Jacob, unlike Esau, desired the birthright and blessing. Knowing the birthright was something for which one could barter in that day, Jacob no doubt planned to do so when the time was right. That day came.

Jacob was cooking red lentil soup. Esau came in from the field, asked to "have a swallow of that red stuff there," and told Jacob he was "famished" (Genesis 25:30). The Hebrew word in this passage isn't the same as in passages where "famished" means "starved." Rather, it means "faint, exhausted, weary."[3] In other words, Esau wasn't about to die. And Jacob had no problem giving Esau a bowl of soup. But first he wanted to talk. Who knows how often the adult twins got together, much less talked about things that were important to them. Jacob seized this moment when he had Esau's attention and got straight to the point: "First, sell me your birthright" (Genesis 25:31).

Esau didn't hesitate: "I am about to die; so of what use then is the birthright to me?" (Genesis 25:32). Since Esau wasn't really a dying man on the brink of starvation, why did he so readily agree to his brother's proposition? Was it because he was confident there was enough wealth to spread to both of them? Did he think he could barter with Jacob at a later time and get it back? Had Isaac assured Esau that regardless of God's proclamation, he would bless him? Or did Esau, the wild child, truly not care about inheriting his father's business, lifestyle, and religion?

Jacob wanted more than a casual agreement from Esau. He insisted, "First swear to me; so he swore to him, and sold his birthright to Jacob" (Genesis 25:33). The next verse concludes, "thus Esau despised his birthright." For Esau to despise his birthright is a strong statement of his lack of character.

Taking Things into Our Own Hands

Genesis 25:34 places no blame on Jacob for acquiring the birthright Esau despised. Up to this point, family relationships have rocked predictably along . . . until Isaac started feeling his age (137) and decided to get his will and testament in order.

Isaac might have succeeded blessing Esau had Rebekah not overheard their conversation. She did, though, and immediately leapt into action, devising a scheme in which Jacob would masquerade as Esau and receive the blessing through deception.

This is wrong. This isn't the same as legally bartering for the birthright, as Jacob had done. This is Rebekah manipulating the situation to accomplish what she wanted for Jacob and believed was God's will. At this point, moms, we have to ask, "Does the end justify the means?" In other words, is it okay to lie to get what we want?

Do we tend "to control or play upon by artful, unfair, or insidious means" to serve our purposes? Again, I'm not referring to rewards for good behavior, such as "If you clean your room, we'll go to the park." Nor am I referring to household rules, as in "Yes, you can move back home, but you'll be expected to go to church with us."

At the heart of Rebekah's plan is distrust in God. It seems she thought if she didn't act, God wouldn't. Nothing would happen like it was supposed to. The prophecy would not come true. In essence, God would be outwitted—His will would be thwarted. She decided she *had* to manipulate the situation to bring about God's will. In effect, she tied God's hands from acting in a divinely remarkable way. In her home, waters weren't parted. Relationships weren't healed. Storms weren't calmed. We don't see God acting in a marvelous way. We see Rebekah teaching her son to scheme to get what he wants. How much better it would have been had she inquired of God, as she had years earlier. What a better model that would have been for Jacob.

What was Jacob's reaction to his mother's manipulative plot? He didn't like it and objected: "I shall be as a deceiver in his [Isaac's] sight, and I shall bring upon myself a curse and not a blessing" (Genesis 27:12). Jacob was concerned, and rightly so. This plot didn't set well with his soul. However, Rebekah forged ahead: "Your curse be on me, my son; only obey my voice, and go, get them for me." So Jacob went and carried out Mom's ploy.

Consequences of Manipulation

Jacob received Isaac's blessing. However, Isaac hadn't genuinely given it. Nor did the deception endear the family members or strengthen relationships. When Esau returned from hunting and went to receive his father's blessing, upon realizing what happened, the old man "trembled violently" (Genesis 27:33). When Esau learned what happened, he cried out "with an exceedingly great and bitter cry" (Genesis 27:34). Esau bore a grudge against Jacob and decided to kill him, so Rebekah sent Jacob away to her brother Laban. Instead of Jacob's being gone a few days, he was gone for years. Rebekah never saw her beloved younger son again. She died not knowing that God had blessed Jacob en route to Haran, accomplishing what He said He was going to do in His way and timing.

Manipulation has consequences. As well-intentioned moms, we do well to think about the negative effects of manipulation, which we don't want to be a part of our relationships.

Loss

When Isaac was tricked into blessing Jacob, did he feel he had, in fact, blessed him? No. Listen to Isaac's explanation to Esau: "Your brother came deceitfully and has taken away your blessing'" (Genesis 27:35).

Recently I was at the courthouse when Keith sentenced a father to life in prison for sexually abusing his daughter. Now, as I read Isaac's lament over what Jacob had "taken away," I'm reminded of how this man and his wife took away their daughter's childhood, modesty, virginity, trust, and so much more. I include the mother in this charge because I cannot believe she was unaware her daughter was being tied to bedposts, repeatedly raped, videotaped, and forced to do what no child should do. Also, the mother had previously manipulated her daughter into recanting her story, telling her the family couldn't survive without the father.

Too often, manipulation is used in families and other relationships. Whether regarding beneficiary or other issues, we must guard our relationships so manipulation doesn't come into play. If we use those means, we'll be guilty of taking away from someone something he or she didn't willingly give.

The following example shows the ripple effect of manipulation on our children.

Bob and I had talked about marriage, but he wasn't ready to commit. I was anxious, though, and called the church to check available dates. Before I knew it, I had booked the church, and we weren't even engaged. I told Bob what I'd done, and he assured me that he wanted to get married but was saving for my ring. I didn't want to wait and convinced him to buy a cubic zirconia. I basically manipulated him into marrying me. Our marriage was a disaster. I was always the one giving. I don't think he ever really wanted to marry me. I never got the "real" diamond. He had an affair. We divorced and now have joint custody of the children. In hindsight I see how

wrong I was and am seeing how important it is not to resort to manipulating people.
I also want to spare my children the results of further manipulation.

Another woman, Sue, shares what it was like to be on the receiving end of manipulation.

My business partner maliciously schemed to empower herself at my expense.
The effects nearly destroyed me and my business. It took years to overcome. I felt
betrayed, robbed, and powerless. I am usually a good judge of people, but I didn't
see this coming. Manipulators are con artists. They are very good at what they do.
Manipulation is intimate because the person plays with your heart, vulnerabilities,
and weakness. It stripped me of my confidence and caused me to have self-doubt
about my ability to know people and hear from God. It weakened my faith some-
what and my ability to trust friends. It didn't just affect me, it affected my family too.

What happens when we use manipulation to get what we want? It doesn't affect just us and the other person involved. It affects our children. It trickles down to them.

Damaged Relationships

Another consequence of manipulation is damaged relationships. Rebekah lost her relationship with her favorite son, Jacob: she never saw him again. Certainly her relationship with Esau was damaged. It's hard to imagine his feelings toward his mother. I can only wonder what Rebekah's trickery did to her relationship with Isaac. We read of them talking and Isaac later blessing Jacob of his own free will. Yet I can't help but wonder if some level of distrust didn't linger in Isaac's mind toward Rebekah.

Resentment

Prior to Rebekah's manipulative actions, we don't have any indication that Esau and Jacob were cross with each other. Yes, they had different interests and occupations. However, they seemed to have a relationship in which Esau would drop by Jacob's home for dinner. The Genesis 25:31–34 account of Esau's selling his birthright to Jacob does not conclude with, "So Esau bore a grudge against Jacob." The Genesis 27:41 account following the deception says just that.

Visit with anyone who has been manipulated, and they will likely express feelings of ill will toward the person who manipulated them. They may bear a grudge for years. Indeed, Rebekah was only kidding herself when she told Jacob she'd send for him after a few days when Esau's "fury subsides, . . . and he forgets what you did to him" (Genesis 27:44–45). Since we have no record that she ever did send for Jacob, it seems Esau's anger didn't subside, nor did he forget after a few days.

Breakup of the Family

Rebekah didn't know, when she concocted the plan to manipulate Isaac into giving Jacob the blessing, that although her plan would succeed, Jacob would suffer the consequences. She had said, "The curse be on me." But it wasn't. Jacob was the one who had to flee for his life. Jacob was the one who ended up living with Laban, being cheated out of Rachel as his only wife, and being cheated of his wages. Their family was literally torn apart as a result of Rebekah's meddling scheme.

And manipulation is still tearing apart families today. Consider my friend Paula's account.

I was two years old the first time I felt the anguish of thinking my mother was dying. I was in the backseat of the car late at night, and Dad was driving her to the hospital. She had overdosed, the first of many times I watched her attempt to take her life. She used suicide attempts to manipulate others to do what she wanted and to gain attention. In my teens I took pills and drank, feeling I wasn't worth my mother wanting to live. Everything revolved around her.

In high school I had a traumatic incidence. The boy I had been dating was killed in a motorcycle wreck. I went into a shell and stayed in bed for days, wondering how I could cope. I had just found out I was pregnant and hadn't had the chance to tell him. When my mother found out, it was all she talked about. One day she and her drinking friend came to school, and I was called over the intercom to come to the office. My mother told them I was being taken out for a medical reason. We drove a hundred miles to the nearest large city for me to have an abortion because Mom said "it was the right thing to do for me not to ruin my life." In the recovery room, as I waited to be released, Mom lay on the couch and sobbed, "Now I'll never become a grandmother." My mother continues to manipulate to gain attention. She waits for me to call or leaves phone messages such as, "Well, I haven't heard from you," and she has a tone—kind of a whine.

Whether we're talking about modern-day mom manipulations or biblical ones, sometimes our response is to say (or at least think), "Why didn't you just pray? Why didn't you wait on God? Why didn't you follow His plan for how to work out your situation? Why did you take things into your own hands?" Honestly, though, can we really say that we never have or never would try to "help things along"?

Moms, how we handle life and relationships is extremely important. Not only are our children watching and learning life skills from us, but they themselves are dramatically affected by our actions.

Learning to Accept God's Way

What can we learn about God through all of this?

First, God is redemptive. He did what He said He was going to do in making Jacob preeminent over Esau. But He did it His way and in His timing. He blessed Jacob and passed the covenant promises through him. In other words, God can take our messes and make them blessings. It may take years. It may not reverse all the suffering and loss we've inflicted. However, God is faithful to forgive us.

Second, God is preemptive. To preempt means to prevent from happening or taking place.[4] God is preemptive in that He wants to prevent us from taking manipulative actions and reaping their destructive consequences. So He takes the initiative and invites us to turn to Him in the face of Plan B difficulties: "Ask, and it will be given to you; seek, and you will find; knock, and it will be opened to you" (Matthew 7:7).

The Bible is filled with examples of how God makes a way when there didn't seem to be a way: the Red Sea parting, the ark saving Noah's family from the flood, Esther saving the Jews. When we manipulate, we're acting in fear, not in faith—in selfishness, not selflessness.

Today, we can choose to turn away from manipulative practices and toward doing things God's way.

LIVE OUT LOUD

Plan A Mom Checkup

Ask yourself the following questions to help you get rid of manipulative behaviors.

1. When faced with a Plan B situation or child, do I try to "fix" the situation or child? Or do I go to God in prayer, ask for His perspective, and follow His direction in how to respond?

2. In the deepest recesses of my mind, do I honestly believe God can provide a way? Do I believe He'll come through in my Plan B situation and with my child?

3. Do I spend more time fretting and talking to others or talking to God about my Plan B circumstance or child?

4. Do I involve my child in my manipulative schemes with others?

5. Do I use any of the following to get what I want, thereby teaching my child to manipulate?

Guilt	"After all I've done for you . . ."
Withdrawal	"If you don't _____ , I'll withhold from you my love, attention, availability . . ."
Bribery	Giving excessive praise, money, or gifts to bring about a desired behavior or to make someone feel obligated to you
Degradation	Cutting words, put-downs, jabs, sarcasm, sneers, dirty looks
Silence	Ignoring, pouting, not answering the phone or returning e-mails
Anger	Slamming doors, phones, yelling
Intimidation	Using threats ("If you don't _____ , you'll be sorry" or "I'll show you") to get what you want
Pity party	"Poor me, no one loves me, I'm all alone, I'm a bad mother, wife, Christian friend . . ."
Helplessness	"If you don't _____ , I'll fall apart, don't know what I'll do . . ."
Crying	Self-induced tears
Time	Being intentionally late or early, stalling
Dress	"I'll wear this to make you want me, not want me, like me, get what I want . . ."

6. Ask God and your children to forgive you for any manipulative behavior of which He convicts you.

7. Look back over the list. Do your children use manipulative behavior? If so, teach them correct ways of relating to you and others. For instance, if Mac sulks because you won't take him to the video store, explain, "Sulking isn't an effective way to get me to do something. Ask me politely, and I'll take you if I can. However, if I can't, please don't sulk. If you feel the need to sulk, please go to your room to do it. I don't want to see it."

8. Begin replacing manipulative behavior with truth, prayer, and God's ways. Model doing things His way. If you don't, I'll feel like a horrible author and cry myself to sleep tonight.

Love Out Loud

1. What might God want you to take to heart regarding Rebekah and manipulation?

2. How was Jacob's bartering with Esau different from what Rebekah did?

3. At one time Rebekah prayed and listened to God. What stands out to you about her lack of prayer in the case of her scheme to get Isaac to bless Jacob?

4. Below write out the words of Psalm 37:5. Try memorizing that verse.

_____

_____

5. What is something you need to commit to the Lord and trust Him for regarding your parenting, children, or Plan B situation?

6. How will having Psalm 37:5 memorized help you in your parenting?

———— ⬥ ————

Between You and God—Principle to Remember

I disarm the land mine of manipulation by doing things God's way.

Father, thank You for showing me the dangers of manipulation. Alert me to any manipulative behaviors my children and I have. Help me to model trusting You rather than *manipulating people and situations. Help me train my children to trust You and do things Your way. In Jesus' name, amen.*

LAUGH OUT LOUD

One day, as we returned home not long after Taylor had first started school, he couldn't get out of the car fast enough. He rushed right into the bathroom. When he reemerged, I asked him why he hadn't gone to the bathroom before he left school. "I don't like to go at school because the toilets are dirty," he replied. "But I've figured out a way to do it if I have to go. I sit on my hands."

My Child or God's Child

I defuse the land mine of thinking my child is mine alone
by remembering that my child is God's child.

*My heart exults in the Lord; My horn is exalted in the Lord. My mouth
speaks boldly against my enemies, because I rejoice in Your salvation.*

1 Samuel 2:1

Hayden clutched the pink rabbit to her chest. "Mine!" the blonde, two-year-old, tousle-headed darling announced to her playmate. When Andrew reached for the toy a second time, Hayden grew more determined. "No, no, NO!"

Clinging to what is ours—or what we perceive to be ours—is as normal as breathing air. We're born with an instinctive desire to hold and protect relationships and possessions. But how does that affect our parenting?

More often than not, we mothers naturally think of our children as *ours*. After all, we're the ones who carry them for nine months. We deliver them. We hold, nurse, feed, diaper, and clothe them. We love on our babies, toddlers, and teens. They look like ours, smell like ours, and walk like ours. Well, at least some of the time. So, aren't they ours?

Ours or God's

Although by all appearances "our" children look like they're ours, the Bible teaches us that children are a gift from the Lord. They originate with Him. They're His idea.

He's their heavenly Father. Children, then, in effect, are an entrustment to us from God. He instructs us to raise them to know Him and walk in His ways. Long after we earthly parents die, our children will be accountable to their heavenly Father.

How can we adopt a "Your child" mentality when our natural attitude is "my child"? What difference would the attitude change make in our daily parenting? We can find the answer to both questions by looking to Hannah.

Dedicated to God in a Plan B Marriage

Hannah was in a less-than-picture-perfect marriage situation, as we have discussed. Her husband had a second wife, so we can imagine how Hannah probably longed to have someone who was hers alone. However, not only did she not have a husband to call her own; she had no child to call her own. How did she handle the heartache of bigamy and barrenness?

Hannah went to the Lord. While worshipping Him, she made a vow: she promised that if He gave her a son, she would dedicate him to God" (1 Samuel 1:11).

What leaps out at us as we read her prayer in the first chapter of 1 Samuel?

Maidservant

First, we can't help but notice how many times Hannah refers to herself as God's maidservant. Thinking of ourselves as a maidservant to the Lord of Hosts in regard to parenting awakens us to a sorely needed divine perspective. One of the greatest ways we can serve God is by raising godly children.

Giving Back

Hannah understands her purpose in life: to serve the Lord of Hosts and His purposes as it relates to her child. Therefore, when Hannah asks God to give her a son, she immediately vows that if He does, she'll give that child to the Lord for all his life.

As I read Hannah's prayer, I can't help but wonder what would happen if more pregnancies began as Hannah's did. I can assure you, when I got pregnant, I wasn't thinking, "If You give me a son, I'll give him back to You all the days of his life." You may have been like Keith and me and simply decided it was time to start a family. Or, you may not have even wanted a child when you became pregnant. You may have been raped or had an unplanned pregnancy. Regardless, we can all learn from

Hannah at whatever stage we find ourselves with our children. We can dedicate our children to God.

Dedication and Worship

In keeping with her vow, when Hannah's son Samuel was weaned at around two to three years of age, she took him to the sanctuary in Shiloh. First Samuel 1:24 seems to make a point of saying, "although the child was young." There they sacrificed at the altar, and Hannah dedicated Samuel to the Lord. First Samuel 1:25–28 also says, "And he worshiped the Lord there."

Who worshiped the Lord? Three-year-old Samuel. How does a three-year-old worship? *Can* a three-year-old worship?

There are several Hebrew words for "worship." The word used in 1 Samuel 1:28 means to bow down, to prostrate oneself before a superior in homage, before God in worship.[1] The visual is Samuel on his knees, bowing to God. No doubt, this was a practice he'd seen his parents often do—similar to how parents teach their children to fold their hands and bow their heads for a blessing over a meal. Likely, some of Samuel's earliest memories were seeing his parents on their knees, bowing to the Lord, praying.

What are (or will be) our children's earliest memories of us? Will they include our being on our knees worshipping the Lord?

Samuel's First Three Years

Children learn by example. We already know from watching Hannah what she's made of. What did young Samuel see?

Hannah, the Faithful

Before Samuel was born, when Peninnah provoked her to tears or Eli wrongly accused her of being drunk, Hannah didn't fight back with sharp retorts. She remained faithful to worship God. She talked to Him. She trusted in the Lord of Hosts, the Lord of armies, the Lord of the angelic realm. She chose to believe that God heard her prayers and acted accordingly. Even her face reflected her faith that God heard her prayers (1 Samuel 1:18), and no doubt Samuel saw that faith in her face, that faithfulness in her life. He would need this model someday when he had to deal with difficult people himself. He learned faith early from his mama.

Hannah, the Preparer

As Hannah modeled godliness for Samuel, I think it's fair to assume she also prepared him for his life in the temple.

When the bull, which they would take to Shiloh to dedicate, was born and growing, did the toddler Samuel run toward it, squealing, as I've seen our grandson do? Did Hannah dash after him and protectively swoop him up in her arms? Did she use that as an occasion to tell him the story of what was to be? "One day, Daddy, Mommy, the bull, and you are going to Shiloh, where the sanctuary of the Lord is. But we can't go until you and the bull are three years old. Then we'll all go together. It'll be a special trip. We'll offer the bull to God for the forgiveness of our sins and have a big feast. Mommy and Daddy will come home, but you'll get to stay at the house of the Lord. Eli, the chief priest, will take good care of you and teach you all about God and serving Him. God has a very special plan for your life."

Hannah, Keeper of Vows

Hannah also taught Samuel that one is to keep his or her vow to God, even at great cost. I can't imagine how difficult it was for Hannah to kiss her little one good-bye and leave him in Shiloh. When our son, Taylor, was three, I had a hard time leaving him at preschool for a few mornings a week!

In addition to her missing Samuel and being concerned about his being homesick, Hannah may have had other concerns about keeping her vow. Eli's sons were worthless men who didn't know the Lord (1 Samuel 2:17), who "lay with the women who served at the doorway of the tent of meeting" (1 Samuel 2:22–24). Hannah had to trust God to keep Samuel pure, uncorrupted by their bad behavior.

Perhaps you've found yourself in a similar position. As a mother you've tried to protect your children, control that to which they're exposed. Yet, if you're divorced, their father, who has joint custody, may have different values than you. Even if you're married and have a stable, godly home, you can't shelter your children from every outside influence.

What would have been a mother's natural response to her son being around men whose sins are described as "great"? She would have feared for their influence on him. However, Hannah appears to have faith that, even though her son is staying in a place where God's laws aren't being observed, God will accomplish His will in Samuel. Hannah rests in the knowledge that she did her part to teach Samuel to honor and serve God. How do we know Hannah isn't weeping or biting her nails as she bids farewell to her only child? We can read what flowed from her heart: "Hannah prayed and said: My heart rejoices in the Lord; in the Lord my horn is lifted high. My mouth boasts over my enemies, for I delight in your deliverance. There is no one holy like the Lord; there is no one besides you; there is no Rock like our God" (1 Samuel 2:1–2 NIV).[2]

Not My Child—God's Child

Hannah had a divine perspective. During Samuel's first three years—those impressionable years when his vocabulary, thoughts, temperament, and personality were being formed—Hannah filled his little ears, eyes, mind, and heart with worship of God.

How did she conduct herself the first night her baby was away from her? On the evidence of her past, we can guess the answer to that question: she was in prayer for her son. She voiced her trust in the Lord. She trusted Him to be Samuel's Rock. She had confidence that the God of the universe would "keep," or watch over, him. Hannah knew God would take care of Samuel.

Another mother, author and speaker Pam Kanaly,[3] found that she could entrust her children to God too. Her testimony echoes Hannah's: that her children are the Lord's.

I recall the snowy Christmas morning in Lubbock, Texas, when I was a young girl. I sat on the steps at five o'clock in the morning at my cousin Rusty's house. We waited in childlike anticipation to see what treasures Santa had left for us under the tree. Our parents called out, "Okay, come and see!" And sure enough, there she was: my long-awaited baby doll. She came in snap-up pajamas, with pink-lidded baby bottles and matching bibs. Her little mouth was opened just enough for me to feed her "real" water. I was totally smitten by her ability to wet her diaper. Indeed, I became a dedicated "mother" when I was five years old.

My mothering activities continued as I grew. I babysat little Mary across the street when I was in late elementary school, and I dreamed of the day I would marry, have my own children, and live happily ever after in my house with the white picket fence.

Mine: I wanted mine. My own husband, my own children, my own house. God gave me that. I married my high-school sweetheart and lived in what I considered my dream-life come true. Then one day, after ten years of marriage, my husband left me in a devastating betrayal when our kids, Jason and Sara, were only two and three years old.

Mothers are naturally possessive anyway, but when they're left as the sole parent in the home, feeling the immense weight of raising healthy children when the household has suddenly become unhealthy, the tendency to clutch them close and assume responsibility for their well-being can become debilitating. After all, we mothers think, if we don't take control, who will? How will they make it in life if we don't make it our job to ensure that they grow into Christ-honoring human beings? And isn't it our role as "mother hawks" to protect their little eyes and ears from any possible dangers?

I recall one weekend when the children returned from spending a few days with their dad. Now, don't get me wrong. He's not a bad person at all; we just had different ideas about what movies the kids could watch. When four-year-old Sara mentioned how much she loved the movie Dirty Dancing with Patrick Swayze, my blood boiled.

What's a mother to do when she's in a situation she can't control or change? How is she supposed to guard her children from harm when they live in a world saturated with images contrary to God's righteousness? Is it possible for her, when she's barely hanging on herself, to parent when all she feels like she can do is provide? At those crisis moments of motherhood, if the principles of God's Word don't take front and center in our thinking, destruction is sure to follow.

A number of destructive land mines were lurking under the surface in my life: Fear—would the children be permanently damaged because of the divorce? Sadness—how could I ever stop loving my former husband and accept the fact that he didn't love me anymore? Bitterness—was it even possible to live with the reality that my children's stepmother would be a woman I counseled at camp when she was ten years old? But most destructive of all, vanity—I believed bringing up these children to be godly adults was solely MY responsibility. I considered them MINE and didn't understand that Jason and Sara were merely entrusted to me for a short while to show them what Christ is like. It was my job to nurture and train; it was God's job to "fix" and bring them to maturity in Him.

Most moms struggle when their children leave the house and go to college. That is a difficult time of letting go, but for me, it was like Jason and Sara "left the *nest" when they were two and three years old. I had to release my grip on them into the hands of their heavenly Father when they left to spend the weekends with their earthly dad. Matthew 7:9 became one of my favorite scriptures: "What man is there among you, when his son shall ask him for a loaf, will give him a stone? Or if he shall ask for a fish, he will not give him a snake, will he? If you, being evil know how to give good gifts to your children, how much more shall your Father who is in heaven give what is good to those who ask Him!"*

More? More? What mother out there doesn't want a dose of God's "more?"

God is the same yesterday, today and tomorrow. And the same God that blessed Hannah and her child is the same God who promises to take care of us and our children. My motherhood motto has become "Not mine, but Thine, oh Lord!"

God has granted His "more" in Pam's life. She's been married to husband Rich now for almost twenty years. And not only did God bless Jason and Sara with healthy lives and godly mates, but He honored Pam in 2010 when she was one of five women nominated by the national organization American Mothers for Oklahoma Mother of the Year.

God's Children Entrusted to Us

We have a responsibility to teach our children about God, His ways, and that obedience brings blessings. How do we do that? We teach them to pray before meals, at bedtime, and in between. We teach them to have thankful hearts.

When Lauren was little, I would take her to the window every morning, look outside, and say, "Thank You, God, for this beautiful day." I had no idea the effect it was having on her until Keith and I went out of town and left the children with their grandparents. Upon returning, one of the first stories Keith's mother told me was that Lauren went to the window, looked out, and said, "Thank You, God, for this beautiful day."

When Taylor was five and Lauren was three, I asked God, "What is the greatest gift I can give my children?" He immediately impressed on my heart to give them the discipline of beginning each day with Him in prayer and Bible reading. "That way, I can take care of them all the days of their lives." My next question was, "How can I make a three- and five-year-old want to come to You first thing every morning?" Again, I felt God answer: "Kidz Time." Then He guided me to develop an easy-to-use, A-to-Z

Plan A Mom Tip

Defuse the land mine of thinking that your child is only your child. Recognize that your child is God's child, whom He loves very much. Dedicate your child to God.

memory verse and devotional activity to do with them when they woke each morning. It was such fun! Taylor, after the fourth morning of Kidz Time, announced that he wanted to choose the verse and set up the activity for the following day. You can imagine how my heart soared. I showed him how to select a verse using the concordance in the back of his Bible. He took it from there.

Have my kids always behaved perfectly? Have I? The obvious answer to both questions is, "Of course not." However, we can help our children establish habits that will help them be dedicated to God.

Live Out Loud

Plan A Mom Checkup

Consider the following to help you root out a "my child" mentality and develop a "God's child" trust.

1. Do I tend to see my child more as mine or more as God's?
2. Have I dedicated my child to God, to serve Him?
3. Although God has given my child to me to raise, how mindful am I each day that the one I'm raising is ultimately God's?
4. How am I daily mentoring my children to be dedicated to God?
5. What portion, verse, or phrase from Hannah's song (1 Samuel 2:1–10) do you want to remember? Pray those words to God, making them your own.

Love Out Loud

1. How does Hannah's dedicating Samuel to God inspire you regarding your children?
2. Hannah recognized she had enemies, as we see in 1 Samuel 2:1. However, on what did she focus?

3. In what specific ways is God calling you to be a better model to your children in terms of being dedicated to God and relating to others on the basis of your dedication to Him?

4. Which words from Hannah's song do you want to flow from your heart?

5. What would a child learn about his or her heavenly Father from a mother from whose heart flowed such words?

Between You and God—Principle to Remember

I defuse the land mine of thinking my child is mine alone by being mindful that my child is God's child, whom He loves very much.

Father, thank You that my children are ultimately Your children, whom You love very much. Help me to be mindful each day that they are Yours. Help me raise them to know, love, and serve You. Protect them when they're away from me. Keep them in Your loving care. In Jesus' name, amen.

Laugh Out Loud

I'm standing at the kitchen sink when I hear Eli (4), who has been sick and whose temperature I've recently taken, pull out a tape measure. After stretching it across my backside, he announces, "99.9". I'm not sure if he was referring to the width of my hips or what he imagined to be my temperature. I going with the latter!—Shellie Dent

6

BEING OVERLY CONTROLLING OR TRUSTING GOD WITH MY CHILD

I defuse the land mine of being controlling
by trusting God.

Trust in the Lord with all your heart and do not lean on your own understanding.
In all your ways acknowledge Him, and He will make your paths straight.

Proverbs 3:5–6

Sarai fiddled about the tents. Looking over the shoulder of a servant who was cooking, she pointed to the cumin. "Add more of that." Not able to rid herself of an ever-increasing edginess, she continued to pace. Children played everywhere. "Why can't I have a baby, God?" she silently cried for the umpteenth time. "How are we to have descendants that number the stars if I can't bear even one?"

Perhaps unfamiliar with not being in control, Sarai struggled with her barrenness. She could handle their many moves. She eventually got over Lot choosing the best land for himself. But this. This had to do with her body and God's promise, and she couldn't "make it happen." Or . . . could she? She pondered. "Maybe, just maybe, God doesn't care if the baby is Abram's and mine or just Abram's. Maybe Abram should sleep with Hagar, and we could raise the baby as our own."

Sarai probably tossed the idea around in her head for days, if not months or years. Finally, she approached her husband. "The Lord has prevented me from bearing children. Please go in to my maid; perhaps I shall obtain children through her. And Abram listened to the voice of Sarai" (Genesis 16:2).

Characteristics of Controlling People

Let's face it: we moms are so used to juggling all the pieces of our lives and our family's lives—organizing, coordinating, making sure everyone's taken care of—that it's easy to slip over the line and control a little more than we should. But where, exactly, is that line? How do you know when you've gone over to the dark side—when you've become one of "those" moms? Let's look at some characteristics of controllers.

Shifting into "Make Things Happen" Mode

When things aren't going according to a controller's plans, she shifts into "make things happen" mode. The less mature we are in our walk with the Lord, the more we do this. Baby believers (identified by their spiritual fruits, not years in the church), who don't have a regular time of prayer, Bible reading, and listening to God, look at a situation before them and "figure out" what to do. Such was the case with Sarai.

Treating People Like Objects

After Abram agreed to Sarai's plan, Genesis 16:3 tells us: "Abram's wife Sarai took Hagar the Egyptian, her maid, and gave her to her husband Abram as his wife."

Although it was a culturally accepted practice for a surrogate to bear children for a barren woman, the Bible gives us no indication that Sarai treated Hagar as anything but an object to be used. The image is of Sarai, wealthy and powerful wife, "taking" Hagar and "giving" her to Abram. Did it matter to Sarai whether Hagar was married, or a virgin? Did Hagar have any say in the matter? Apparently not.

Even when the all-powerful God selected Mary to bear Jesus, we sense a gracious pause during which the young virgin willingly consented to God's choice of her to bear His Son. Not so, it seems, with Sarai and Hagar.

Using God's Words to Justify Behavior

Controlling people often are religious. They know God's Word—and how to use it to justify their behavior while disregarding its full counsel and intent. This is what Sarai did. She took seriously God's words that their descendants would number more than the stars; however, she disregarded the possibility that God could honor His promise without her intervention.

Dangers of Being Controlling

Sarai stands as a warning. Yes, we may be able to control people and things. We may even obtain an outcome that initially seems satisfactory. But time will prove that God's ways are the right ways. Obeying some of His commands while disregarding others will not bring forth His best in our lives. In fact, we can do a lot of damage. What are some of the dangers of being controlling?

Being Despised

It doesn't take fourteen chapters or even four verses for us to see the negative consequences of Sarai's "controlled" birth plan. Abram had sexual relations with Sarai's maid, and Genesis 16:4 tells us that "when she [Hagar] saw that she had conceived, her mistress was despised in her sight."

The Hebrew word translated "despised" here means to be slight, trifling, of little account, insignificant, lightly esteemed, to treat with contempt or dishonor.[1] Hagar the maid is now looking down her nose at Sarai her mistress. We can envision Hagar with her tummy growing, gloating about the tent. She hadn't wanted to be treated like an object and forced to lay with old Abraham. Yet Sarai had demanded it. "Now how do you like it?" Hagar must have thought as saw the yearning in Sarai's eyes.

Blaming Others

When controllers' plans don't work out, they're quick to blame and find fault in others. Sarai doesn't like Hagar's attitude, but she takes no ownership of the complications in their relationship. Instead, she blames the whole mess on Abram. "It's your fault that Hagar despises me. I myself gave her to you, and ever since she found out that she was pregnant, she has despised me. May the Lord judge which of us is right, you or me" (Genesis 16:5 GNT).[2]

Not only does Sarai deny any responsibility—she wants Abram to get in the middle of the situation. Abram refuses: "Your maid is in your power; do to her what is good in your sight" (Genesis 16:6).

Becoming More Controlling

What did Sarai do to mend her relationship with Hagar? Nothing. As a matter of fact, Sarai treated her harshly to the point that Hagar fled. As a servant, Hagar probably wasn't even sure where she was going or how she would live—she just knew she had to get out from under Sarai's controlling reign.

Left at home with no maid and no baby, Sarai found herself in a mess. We would like to think Sarai used this time to consider her actions and change. She didn't.

Burdening Others

Sarai's controlling behavior brought burdens on others. Hagar was burdened with an unwanted pregnancy. She was burdened under harsh treatment. She was burdened in the wilderness when she fled from her mistress. Even though she returned, she would be burdened again, years later, when Sarai drove her and her son Ishmael out. We can't imagine the burden she must have felt thinking she would have to watch her child die.

Ishmael was burdened with a single mother and abandoned in the wilderness with no food or water. He would have died had God not pointed his mother to water. The Muslim people trace their roots to Abraham through the blood line of Ishmael. The burden continues.

Factors That Contribute to Our Being Controlling

Okay, so we all agree being controlling is bad. How, then, do we avoid becoming controllers? Or, if we already see a little too much Sarai in the mirror, how did we get this way? We can start to change our controlling ways—or avoid falling into them—by understanding what leads to them in the first place.

Not Trusting God

At the root of our controlling nature is lack of trust in God. We look at a situation and think we must act. We must make a person do something or make a thing happen. If we don't, we think the desired outcome won't occur. We force our kids to play sports because we fear they won't learn the value of teamwork if they don't. We fail to trust God that they can learn good team values in a drama department, debate competition, choir, or band. We make our children dress a certain way, even if it isn't their taste or style. We fail to trust that God knows what He's doing when He makes each child unique.

Fear

Fear is a close relative to not trusting God. We fear that if we don't have control over another person, thing, or event, bad things will happen. If our child isn't ready to start kindergarten, we worry what others will think if we hold him back a year. We try to make our active little boy sit still when the best thing for him may be to climb trees and explore outside. We try to force our daughter to be potty trained when she's not yet conscious of her bodily needs. We shame her for accidents rather than praise her for her successes. We overreact or become angry when our children test us rather than realizing that it's natural for them to push the limits and that the best thing we can do is remain lovingly consistent.

Operating in the Flesh

Another reason we often resort to controlling behavior is that we're operating in the flesh rather than in Christ's Spirit. Galatians 4:21–31 clearly states that Ishmael's birth was an act of the flesh. Contrast that with Isaac's birth, which was an act of the Spirit. In other words, Sarai "made it happen" for Abraham to have a child. She did it by forcing Hagar to lie with him. God was shoved out of the picture. Sarai's fleshly actions resulted in fleshly consequences: Hagar despised her. Ishmael taunted Isaac. Muslims and Jews continue to be enemies.

Biblical Solutions for the Controlling Nature

Moms, do we control situations or our children and then end up not liking the result? Do our kids or our spouses ever become resentful, like Hagar did, over our attempts to control them? Or, like Abram, do they want nothing further to do with us and the mess we've created?

Abram made an astute comment: "Your maid is in your power." To a great extent, our children are in our power. How can we make sure we operate in the Spirit rather than in the flesh?

Take your thoughts to God

If Sarai had taken her thoughts captive to God's commandments, she would have known that giving her maid to her husband was not a good idea. What are we supposed to do when we don't like our Plan B barrenness, our Plan B child, their Plan B situation or ours? We're to go to God. We're to take our thoughts captive and bring them into submission to His will. We're to model to our children that just because what we wanted didn't occur or hasn't happened in our timing, it's not the end of the world. Perhaps God has a different plan.

When Lauren was a cheerleader in middle school, she tried out to be a Freshman cheerleader the next year in high school. She didn't make it. Immediately, all sorts of thoughts flooded her mind. "What if I can't make friends? What if I don't have anyone to hang out with?" Needless to say, my heart broke for my daughter, and of course I thought she should have made it. What mother doesn't? However, I also had a few years of spiritual maturity on her and knew in my heart that God was in control. I was able to pray with her and remind her that, earlier, we had prayed that *if it was God's will*, she would make the cut. I helped her take her thoughts captive by speaking the truth: God would help her make friends. This was not the end of the world. God had wonderful plans for her. She could trust Him.

As moms we have the opportunity to model for our children that, try as they might, they can't control all the outcomes in their lives. But they can pray and take their fearful or negative thoughts to God when they're disappointed or discouraged.

Lean not on your own understanding

Proverbs 3:5–6 encourages us, "Trust in the Lord with all your heart and do not lean on your own understanding. In all your ways acknowledge Him, and He will make your paths straight." If we would take that counsel to heart, we and our children would be much better off. Just because Sarai couldn't understand God's timing, that didn't justify her leaning on her own understanding—which, as rational as it seemed at the time, was contrary to God's. Had she instead acknowledged God and trusted Him, her path and the paths of others would have been strewn with less pain and suffering.

Life will present us with situations that tempt us to take control. But what a better lesson for our kids if we instead say, "I don't know why. . . . However, we can trust God. His ways are higher than ours. God is good and has a plan for our lives."

In all your ways acknowledge God

Plan B's are going to happen. We live in a fallen world. We are sinful by nature. Our children are imperfect. Those with whom we live and relate are imperfect. However, if we acknowledge God, our lives will be infused with His Spirit and blessings rather than infected with our fleshly messes. What does it mean to acknowledge God? The Hebrew word used in Proverbs 3:6 means "to perceive and see, find out and discern;

to discriminate, distinguish; to know by experience; have knowledge, be wise."[3] Every time we open the Bible to learn more about God and His ways, we are choosing to become more discriminate, perceptive mothers. This is a trait our children deserve and our God demands. His Word tells us to "Study to show yourself approved" (2 Timothy 2:15). How good are you at obeying God's instruction: in all your ways acknowledge God; in all your ways perceive and see; in all your ways find out and discern; know God by experience?

An Interview with Thelma Wells

A few months ago I had the privilege of spending time with Thelma Wells, founder of A Woman of God Ministries[4], author, and Women of Faith speaker. During the course of our conversation and discussion about this book, she commented that trusting God with her daughter far outweighed what she could have accomplished by being controlling. Following is part of our discussion.

Debbie: *Thelma, did you ever have a time in your mothering experience when you wanted to control who your daughter was, what she did, how she talked, what her interests were, or how she related to people?*

Thelma: Yes, because I wanted her to exhibit my personality and be upbeat and social all the time. However, she enjoyed reading, being alone, and not being the belle of the ball like me.

Debbie: *What was the result when you tried to control her?*

Thelma: One day I got sick and tired of introducing her to people and her acting like she wasn't interested in meeting them. I scolded her for being what I considered rude. (Her typical reply to meeting someone was a terse "Hi.")

Debbie: *What caused you to finally give up controlling her and entrust her to God?*

Thelma: After I chastised her about not speaking as I thought she should have, it didn't seem to bother her at all. In fact, she taught me a great lesson when she replied, "Mama, I'm not you. I love you, but I don't want to be like you." I let my feelings be hurt over that statement, but after I got over being subjective and became objective, I understood what she was saying. She meant that she was an individual with her own personality, desires, etc., and she needed me to respect her individually. This made

	me realize that no two people are alike. God made each of us special, and we should respect His creation and not judge it or try to change it.
Debbie:	*What was the result?*
Thelma:	The result was that I stopped trying to mold her in my image and accepted her for who God made her to be. My other children didn't have to deal with me trying to make them over. God does His best work when He creates us. We have an obligation to respect His creation.
Debbie:	*Tell us about your daughter and what she's doing today.*
Thelma:	Today she runs A Woman of God Ministries, the ministry God has entrusted to me. She does a fantastic job because her skills and mine are different. She is analytical, precise, accurate, intuitive, and creative. She's a marketing guru, planner, and implementer. She wrote, produced, and directed our performance of the play *The King Sisters*. She's just what I need to make the ministry run correctly and smoothly.
Debbie:	*What advice do you have for moms who are trying to control who and what their children are?*
Thelma:	Train up your child in the way he or she should go, and don't worry about the differences among them and their siblings. Accept each child's personality. Study their interests, talents, and skills and encourage them to pursue what they enjoy. Don't compare one child with another, because each has his or her own personality (soul) that must be developed. Don't push your children in things for which they have little aptitude. Encourage them in what they enjoy. As they become adults, show them and teach them the right way to go, but remember, if you don't want anyone controlling you, don't do it to them.

What a wise woman Thelma was to listen to her daughter and process what she was saying to her when she said she loved her but wasn't like her. What happens when we don't pause to contemplate whether we're being controlling? Consider the following answers I received from people when I asked, "Did you have a controlling parent? Are you one? What effect has it/does it have on you/your child?"

I had a very controlling mom. I ended up getting married one week after I turned eighteen to someone just as controlling as she was, which didn't help my super-low self-esteem. I was abused by my now ex-husband. Controlling moms are terrible. I love my mom, but I live two thousand miles from her.—Donna

My philosophy was to set boundaries as wide as possible, to give my kids as much freedom as I could, but to enforce the boundaries consistently. I watched other parents who had longs lists of rules they never enforced. It appeared to me that both the children and the parents were frustrated.—Suzanne

The goal is to move from control (not letting a two-year-old run in the street or make all of his own food choices) to influence as a child becomes more verbal. That's the Deuteronomy emphasis on training.—Deana Blackburn

Needless to say, mothers are expected to exercise reasonable control over their children. It's not okay for one child to hurt another. It's not okay for a child to talk back to a parent or say unkind things to another. We pick up our toddlers who are headed toward danger. We control their environment to prevent them from being hurt. We control our children's bedtime. We set rules like these: We brush our teeth. We take our plates from the table to the dishwasher. We hang up our clothes rather than drop them on the floor. We make our beds. We put away our toys after we play with them. We do our chores. We go to church. We do our homework. We say "Thank you" and "Please."

However, you might be a controlling mom if . . .

- You insist your child wear the exact color shirt you like instead of the color he chooses.
- You don't let your child have the horse comforter for his bed because you like the cow comforter.
- Your child asks for orange juice, but you make her drink apple juice.
- Your child asks to watch *VeggieTales* A, but you insist on watching *VeggieTales* B.
- Your child wants a blue bike, but you say he gets a black bike or none at all.
- Your child wants to play basketball, but you make him play football.
- Your daughter wants to take tap lessons, but you make her take ballet.

- Your child wants to take a shop class, but you make him take an art class.

I think you get the point. Someone once wisely advised me, "Major in the majors and minor in the minors." I appreciate the advice. It led me to pause and question whether the thing I wanted to enforce was a matter of importance or simply my preference. So, if your child wants to take a walk and you want to ride your bicycle, why not ride circles around her on the walk?

Plan A Mom Tip

Defuse the land mine of being overly controlling. Practice trusting God and looking to Him in your Plan B moments.

Sarai was a controlling woman. May we pause and consider whether we're more controlling than we need to be. Let us be wise and follow God's counsel: "Trust in the Lord with all your heart and do not lean on your own understanding. In all your ways acknowledge Him, and He will make your paths straight."

LIVE OUT LOUD

Plan A Mom Checkup

Plan A moms, often motivated by love, try to control their children and their situations. No doubt, Sarai thought she was doing the right thing when she gave Hagar to Abram. However, her red flag should have been that she was acting outside of God's divine principles. The biblical account includes no reference to her praying about her decision. Rather, since God's timing didn't align with hers, she attempted to take control of the situation. In the end, however, she couldn't control outcomes—and neither can we. When we try, we often end up in a worse situation—even driving loved ones away from us.

If you're prone to control rather than trust, take a moment to evaluate this land mine. Prayerfully choose to defuse it.

1. Do you tend to become angry when things don't go your way?

2. When others don't behave like you want them to, do you use any of the following means to control them?
   - ☐ Pouting or sulking
   - ☐ Raising your voice
   - ☐ Withholding favors
   - ☐ Giving "the look"
   - ☐ Refusing to cooperate
   - ☐ Putting them down
   - ☐ Nagging
3. If you tend to be more naturally controlling than trusting, repent. Ask God to alert you when you're slipping into control mode.
4. Memorize Proverbs 3:5–6.
5. Apologize to those who have borne the brunt of your controlling behavior.

LOVE OUT LOUD

1. Read Genesis 16:1–6. Do you recognize any of Sarai in yourself? Would others say they recognize a touch of Sarai in you?
2. Read Genesis 21:1–7. What message can you take to heart as a mother in light of this passage and Isaiah 55:8–9?
3. Sometimes, although we rejoice in the blessings of God's faithful workings in our lives, we still have to deal with the consequences of our past efforts to usurp control over a person or situation, rather than letting God be in control, as evidenced in Genesis 21:8–10. What do we see Abraham doing in Genesis 21:11–14 that isn't recorded in Genesis 6:1–6? *Hint: To whom did Abraham listen, and how did he get involved?*
4. What do you most need to do in response to Proverbs 3:5–6? How will acknowledging God vastly improve your relationships with your children and others?
5. In what way do Thelma Wells' comments cause you to stop and examine your parenting practices?
6. What encouragement do you receive from Thelma's comments?

Genesis 21:6 records that Sarah laughed. No doubt she experienced many days of not laughing, of heartache and grief over her failed efforts at control. Yet over and above all of her mistakes, God was faithful to Sarah. He'll be faithful and gracious to you too. Take a moment now and record every single thing you can think of for which you are thankful. For instance, can you see? Can you feel? Are you able to walk? Do you have a roof over your head? Do you have children? Is a door open for you to model unselfishness and trusting God before them? Make a list. Give yourself a break. Laugh with God over the good He has brought into your life. Join Paul in saying, "I do not regard myself as having laid hold of it yet; but one thing I do: forgetting what lies behind and reaching forward to what lies ahead, I press on toward the goal for the prize of the upward call of God in Christ Jesus" (Philippians 3:13–14).

BETWEEN YOU AND GOD—PRINCIPLE TO REMEMBER

I defuse the land mine of being controlling by trusting God with my child.

Father, thank You for the reminder that Your ways are higher than my ways. Help me to trust You rather than lean on my own understanding. Help me let go of the minor things and major in that which has eternal value. Thank You for forgiving me of my sins and giving me new opportunities with You and my children. In Jesus' name, amen.

LAUGH OUT LOUD

When Morgan was about three, I decided to try the disciplinary method of lightly spanking with a wooden spoon when she needed correcting. One morning we were in the kitchen together, and I said, "Morgan, this is a wooden spoon, and when you need correcting for something, I'm going to lightly tap you on your hand with this spoon." She said, "Oh, no, Mommy, that 'poon isn't for 'panking—it's for 'tirring! Needless to say, I found a different kind of discipline.—Jeri Sprouse

Tomorrow or Today

I defuse the land mine of procrastination
by teaching my child about God today.

*These words, which I am commanding you today, shall be on your heart. You shall
teach them diligently to your sons and shall talk of them when you sit in your house
and when you walk by the way and when you lie down and when you rise up.*

Deuteronomy 6:6–7

If you've been putting off the daily teaching of God's Word to your children, today is the day to start. Why? God commands you to. Why? So your children learn how to follow Christ in a Plan B world. Because your child's best defense against his carnal nature, temptation, and false gods is to have God's Word in his heart (Psalm 119:11). And because you don't know if you have tomorrow.

Hannah knew the brevity of time she had to spiritually impact her son Samuel. Although his growing up in the temple with the high priest Eli might sound ideal, Hannah knew better—as we've already mentioned, Eli's sons were evil men who didn't know the Lord, despised the offering of the Lord, and lay with the women who served at the doorway of the tent of meeting (1 Samuel 2:12, 17, 22).

How would you like your three-year-old living in that environment? Welcome to Hannah's world. We might as well add, welcome to our world. Too often our children are exposed to violence, sex, and disrespectful behavior and language their pure minds shouldn't hear or see. Whether through media or real-life examples, they observe worldly values and relationships. Is it any wonder our kids treat us and others disrespectfully? It's time for us to wake up and protect our children.

Getting Over the Hump

Have you ever felt that your parenting responsibilities are an albatross? You know you should have daily devotions with your children but don't get around to it. You mean to have one-on-one time with your kids to discuss their day and mentor them in God's ways, but e-mails and phone calls press in on you. You have every intention of praying more specifically and intentionally for your children, but a hurried "God, bless them" is as far as you get.

What are our responsibilities in relation to our children's spiritual education? Is it enough to take them to church or enroll them in a Christian school?

As a mom, you are in a position to influence your children as no one else can. Your kids' teachers at church or school are with them for a limited time and within a specific framework. You're the one who brought your children into this world (or adopted them), and you're responsible for them. Just as we physically feed our children, so we must spiritually feed them. This isn't an added burden to our day. Rather, it's what God means when He says, "These words . . . shall be on your heart. You shall teach them diligently" (Deuteronomy 6:6–7). We're to teach our children about God during the natural course of the day. We don't have to beat them over the head with the Bible, but we can weave God's teachings into present situations and challenges rather than compartmentalizing them into one hour, one day of the week.

When we talk, what do we talk about? We talk about what's on our minds. What's on our minds? The answer is, what fills our hearts. Jesus explained, in Matthew 15:19, that "out of the heart come evil thoughts." Thoughts, whether evil or holy, come from our heart. That's why Deuteronomy 6:6 says, "These words, which I am commanding you today shall be on your heart." If God's Word is in our heart, it will naturally flow from our mouths.

The word *be* means to exist, to live. The Hebrew word translated "heart" in this verse means "inner part, soul, mind, thinking, reflection, memory, inclination, resolution, determination of will, conscience."[1] Thus, God's commands are to live in our soul, to be present in our mind, to exist in our thinking and be part of our conscience and determination of will. Why is this so important? Because the few scriptures we hear on a given Sunday can easily be forgotten in the midst of a child's temper tantrum, a teen's emotional meltdown, or a last-minute science project. However, if God's words are in our heart, then our parenting will flow from a spiritual place— one of love, patience, and kindness rather than the impatience or frustration of our fallen human nature.

Filling Your Heart

How can we make sure God's words are present in our hearts every day, driving our thoughts and behavior? We can daily soak in God's Word. We can ask God to fill us with His Spirit and with the mind of Christ.

To help us understand the need to saturate our hearts and minds with God's Word, consider a sponge. If a sponge is dry, nothing can be squeezed out of it. Many times, we can be like a dry sponge. We walk past our Bible on our way to the kitchen to start the coffeemaker. We turn on the television and check the weather instead of checking the Scriptures. We dress our bodies but not our hearts. When the baby cries, the toddler knocks cereal on the floor, and our teen enters the room dressed inappropriately, our dry-sponge soul cracks. We have nothing to give out but frustration and harsh words.

But what if that sponge had been refreshed with clean running water? A soul soaked in Living Water would have something better to offer.

Just like a sponge, our minds and hearts pick up dirt every day. We desperately need to place ourselves under the fresh cleansing flow of the Holy Spirit. We need washing. We need to be filled with Christ's Spirit. That's God's command and the only way we can parent as He requires: with a heart that has His Words and commands written on it.

If you think you can effectively parent according to Deuteronomy 6:6–7 without daily soaking in God's Word, I challenge you to the sponge test. Use a sponge to wipe your counters and clean the sink, but don't rinse it. The next morning, use that dry, dirty sponge to clean the spilled milk and wipe the peanut butter off the counter. Again, don't rinse it. How effectively will your dry, yucky sponge work on the next cleanup job?

When we don't spend time with God, confessing and repenting of our bad attitude, despair, misgivings, or resentment, we'll carry those feelings into the next day and the day after. Our hearts will be a far cry from overflowing with God's words and commands. Not only will we not be talking about God and His ways with our children, we'll be teaching them the world's ways of acting, thinking, holding onto anger, and living in despair.

Are you a stinky sponge straining to squeeze a bit of Jesus onto your children? Or is your heart a clean, Spirit-filled sponge pouring Christ into your child's life?

The good news is, this doesn't have to be hard. Here are some things I do to fill my heart—I hope they'll help you too.

1. Upon waking, I direct my thoughts toward God. "Thank You, God, for this day. Use me to serve You." This choice of will and act of obedience to be thankful in all things is important. Otherwise I can fall into a state of despair and self-centeredness: "I wish I could stay in bed longer. How will I get everything done today? I wish the baby would sleep longer. I wish I didn't have to go to work."

2. After turning on the coffeemaker on my way to my study, I kneel before God, again directing my thoughts heavenward, praising Him for who He is. Sometimes the praise flows from my need. If I feel weak or not up to the task before me, I might say, "Thank You, God, that You are strong. You are sufficient. You are everything I need." Such praise pleases my Father because it communicates my trust in Him. It affirms that I'm not going to whine as if I had no heavenly Father and Helper. It shows that I realize I'm not up to the task but am confident that Christ in me is capable. Other times my praise flows from a verse or passage of Scripture: 2 Samuel 22 is a favorite because it's filled with God's attributes, as are Psalms and Isaiah. I also use *365 Names, Titles, and Attributes of God*,"[2] my personal collection of God's attributes with Scripture references.

3. By this time I'm soaking in God's presence. My dry soul is filling with the reality of who God is. For instance, as I turn in my Bible and read Hannah's words when she left toddler Samuel at the temple, my faith swells. "My heart exults in the Lord; . . . I rejoice in Your salvation. . . . There is no one holy like the Lord, ... nor is there any rock like our God . . . for the Lord is a God of knowledge" (1 Samuel 2:1–3). (There it is—He can help me with what to do about my child!)

4. I continue to P.R.A.Y. (Praise, Repent, Ask, Yield).[3] I pray for my husband, children, and others, often focusing on God's attribute for which I praised Him. (See "Pray with Purpose, Live with Passion" in the appendix at the end of this book.)

After soaking in God's presence, I'm ready to drip a few words of kindness on my children. When I'm under pressure, patience, not anger, is squeezed out of me. Oh, of course, I'm going to run dry or something is going to throw me off during the day, or especially in the evening, when I'm tired. However, knowing that I tend to run dry, I can be intentional about soaking in God's presence in additional ways.

5. Music is powerful. Knowing it affects my mind and my countenance, I often listen to Christian music in my car and when I come home from a hard day. Why? I find truth to combat negative thoughts. I find uplifting refrains that set my soul straight. It fills my dry spirit and prepares me for my parenting responsibilities, whether I'm babysitting a toddler or visiting with an adult child. To know the powerful effect of Christian music and not take advantage of it is downright silly, in my opinion.

6. Christian books, Bible studies, DVDs, podcasts, and television and radio programs are additional tools I use to saturate my heart with God's words.

7. Christian friends are another resource I turn to when my soul needs replenishing. Although conversations with others don't compare to the ocean of God's presence, they are like a refreshing shower. Friends who are filled with God's Spirit sprinkle truth and life as they speak. Their words bless, encourage, and exhort.

8. Continual conversation with the Father and re-reading the Bible are the mainstays of how I keep my heart saturated with His words and commands. The more I meditate on Him, the more my mind is transformed rather than conformed to our Plan B world (Romans 12:1–2).

If God's Words and commands live in our hearts and minds, then the second part of the instruction in Deuteronomy 6:6–7, teaching diligently, comes naturally.

Teaching Diligently

"These words, which I am commanding you today, shall be on your heart. You shall teach them diligently" (Deuteronomy 6:6).

The words and commands we receive from the Lord are to remain on our hearts in a way that affects us. Because we're affected by what God teaches us, we, in turn, can affect our children.

Why is it important to diligently teach our children?

The answer is found in Deuteronomy 6:12–24. If we don't, our children can forget the Lord and end up following the gods of the people around them. Also, we should teach them God's ways so it will be well with them and they can take hold of what God has given them—it is for their good, even their survival.

Perhaps you've heard, "We're one generation from extinction." Certainly, the Bible demonstrates that we can't assume the next generation will "catch" our faith. Eli's sons were worthless and sinful. David's son, Absalom, rebelled. The Old Testament is filled with godly kings whose sons rejected God. Children must be taught so they will know what they believe and why. They must see our faith modeled. "Faith comes by hearing and hearing by the word of Christ" (Romans 10:17) coupled with "Let your light shine before men in such a way that they may see your good works, and glorify your Father who in heaven" (Matthew 5:16) is a good formula for raising children to know and love the Lord.

What does it mean to diligently teach our children?

To teach diligently means to sharpen, whet, teach incisively, pierce.[4] In other words, we're to teach with perception, judiciously, and thoughtfully, in both a systematic way and also according to the needs of the moment. It's teaching that's applicable and pierces our children's souls rather than rolling off their backs.

Kamal Saleem, a former terrorist who is now a Christian, warns believers that while their children are watching television, mothers in extremist factions of Islam are diligently teaching their children their philosophies. He recalls how his mother taught him to be a radical jihadist.

It was at my mother's kitchen table, surrounded by the smells of herbed olive oils and pomegranates, that I first learned of jihad. Every day, my brothers and I gathered around the low table for madrassa, our lessons in Islam. Mother sat at the head of the table and read to us from the Koran and also from the hadith, which records the wisdom and instruction of Allah's prophet, Muhammad. I vividly remember the day in madrassa when we heard the story of a merciless bandit who went about robbing caravans and killing innocent travelers. "This bandit was an evil, evil man," Mother said, spinning the tale as she sketched pictures of swords for us to color.

An evil bandit? She had my attention.

"One day, there was a great battle between the Jews and the sons of Islam," she went on. "The bandit decided to join the fight for the cause of Allah. He charged on a great, black horse, sweeping his heavy sword left and right, cutting down the infidel warriors."

My eyes grew wider. I held my breath so as not to miss a word.

"The bandit fought bravely for Allah, killing several of the enemy until the sword of an infidel pierced the bandit's heart. He tumbled from his horse and died on the battlefield."

"After the bandit died," Mother was saying in her storytelling voice, "his mother had a dream. In this dream, she saw her son sitting on the shore of an endless crystal river, surrounded by a multitude of women who were feeding him and tending to him."...

My mother swept her eyes around the kitchen table. "So you see, my sons, even the most sinful man is able to redeem himself with one drop of an infidel's blood."[5]

"It is your duty," she said. "It is the duty of the faithful to punish and harass the Jews and Christians, who are as thieves and traitors to Islam. They are cursed as monkeys and pigs, and their spirits are unclean. It is in the Book."[6]

Today's Christian mom wants to provide her children with "the best." However, our children won't be destroyed for lack of clothing, sports, or cell phones. Rather, the threatening cause of destruction is lack of knowledge of God. "My people are destroyed for lack of knowledge. Because you have rejected knowledge, I also will reject you from being My priest. Since you have forgotten the law of your God, I also will forget your children" (Hosea 4:6).

There is no greater gift you, God's priest (1 Peter 2:9), can give your children than knowledge of God's Word and ways. Equipped with knowledge, your children can stand against false religions and Satan's temptations and stand for truth, excellence, and holiness.

How can we diligently teach our children?

Teaching our children doesn't have to be stiff and formal. Kamal Saleem's mother taught him by telling stories as he sat coloring pictures at the kitchen table. The most effective teaching parents can do happens in normal, everyday settings, as we do normal, everyday things. Deuteronomy 6:6–7 gives us several suggestions for how to go about this: "These words, which I am commanding you today, shall be on your heart. You shall teach them diligently to your sons and shall talk of them when you sit in your house and when you walk by the way and when you lie down and when you rise up." Let's take a closer look.

"When you sit in your house"

Consider the following stages and ways you can teach your children when you sit in your house.

In utero. When pregnant with Taylor, I was fascinated to learn that he could hear and recognize my voice.[7] With that knowledge, I sang hymns to my children, read my Bible aloud, and told them I loved them. Why wait until after they're born? Isn't it wonderful? Moms have the power to be the first influencers in our children's lives. We can make sure their untouched, pure minds are first touched with the sound of God's love for them.

Infants. What a joy it was to hold Taylor and Lauren and nourish them at my breast. Equally joyful was nourishing them with God's Word. I discovered that rather than say I didn't have time for morning devotions due to nursing at wee hours in the morning, I could read my Bible and pray over my little ones during that time. I sang lullabies with Christian lyrics and prayed over them when they cried. Sure, I also pulled out my hair sometimes. But that goes with the territory.

Toddlers. The toddler years are a golden time to help your little one develop a love for Bible stories. Keep in mind, you're establishing lifelong habits for your child. Just as you teach the routine of brushing teeth, you can teach the routine of beginning each day with a Bible story. Let your child hold the Bible and turn the pages. Point out pictures of Noah, Joseph, David, Mary, and Jesus. Talk about how God loved them and told them what to do; how they obeyed God, and God took care of them. Make it a fun part of your daily routine.

Preschool and kindergarten. As I mentioned before, *Kidz Time*[8] was a favorite of ours when Taylor was five and Lauren was three. Lauren would read the letter of the alphabet. Taylor read the verse. Both highlighted the verse in their Bible with a yellow crayon. I wanted them to know that the words they were learning and enjoying were from the Bible. It's important for our children to understand that our behavior and words should be checked against the Bible. Help your kids develop that understanding and practice. For instance, if a child says, "Jeremy talks mean to his brother, and his mommy lets him," share Ephesians 4:32. Let your child read the verse aloud: "Be kind to one another."

School age and teens. As the children grew, we adopted different methods of teaching God's Word to them. I can't emphasize enough the importance of family meals. Your family may consist of you and one child. Or it may be you, your husband, and seventeen children. Regardless, I believe a sit-down meal at least once a day should be the norm rather than the exception. Much more than consuming food happens when families eat together. Mom, come away from the kitchen stove and sit down with your kids. Look them in the eye and smile at them. Tell them, "I love you, and so does God." Sitting down with our children tells them they're important. It also provides an opportunity for you to model spiritual practices, such as bowing our heads to give thanks to God.

In addition to teaching gratefulness and showing our children they're valuable and worth our time to sit and visit with them over a meal, we can use mealtime to teach God's commands in a natural, nonconfrontational way. Keith and I used age-appropriate devotional readings each day. When you raise children this way from infancy, it's simply a normal part of their life.

Adult children. You may think that once your children are out of the house, your time of teaching them God's Word has ended. Now that our children are grown, our relationship with them is one of "sharing" more than overt teaching. They know I'm always open to a discussion. However, I often like to reply to their spiritual questions with, "What do you think?" It's fun to watch them continually learn and grow. If you haven't been overbearing with your teaching in their childhood and have a good relationship with your adult children, you may find open doors to continue loving on your kids with the Scriptures. For example, I forward a verse to my children every morning. With all the other e-mails they receive, I'm glad they get that encouragement along with the "I love you" I add. It's a blessing to see which passages scratch where one of them itches. Taylor may fire back a thought-provoking doctrinal question. Ali or Chris may reply, "This was just what I needed today," or Lauren may send a simple, "I love you, Mommy." Or, I may not receive any reply, and that's okay too.

"When you walk by the way"

We're also to teach our kids when we walk through our everyday lives. Jesus is our model for teaching about God in the natural course of our day, making spiritual application in things as simple as seeds or rocks.

If our son comes home from baseball practice disheartened because he didn't do well, we can encourage him that God knows his sorrows and that he can pray about anything. We might say, "I'm sorry you had a bad day. Jesus knows what it's like to have a bad day. Remember, you can talk to Him about everything. As a matter of fact, Philippians 4:6 says to tell God your needs and not to forget to thank Him for His answers. Let's pray right now and ask God to help you be the best baseball player you can be."

If we have God's Word in our hearts, Christian teachings will flow naturally and in an encouraging way.

Playing Christian music in the car is another fun and pleasant way to be mindful of God's Word. When Taylor and Lauren were young, we listened to Psalty's kids' songs. We, myself included, learned about friendship, kindness, not being argumentative, sharing, forgiveness, and more. The music was uplifting, and as we memorized the lyrics, we memorized God's Word.

As Taylor and Lauren got older, they experimented with different music, which we allowed them to do. When rock music became popular with Taylor and his friends, Petra recordings found their way into our home. Although I didn't like them at first, I learned to. It was important to give in to some of Taylor's preferences so he could mature and become the man God called him to be. He certainly wasn't supposed to always like what I liked. The test was in the words; we could be flexible about the beat. I ended up jogging to Petra.

When Lauren came home from a Christian camp one summer, she was anxious for me to listen to a song. "You're going to love it!" she said, handing me her DVD player. Plopping down in the chair, I placed her earphones in my ears. Upon first hearing the song, it didn't grab me. I continued listening, realizing the song was important to Lauren. Then, as I concentrated on the words and sensed the musician's passion for God, I liked it. Today I close every P.R.A.Y. with Passion Conference signing to the song my daughter introduced me to: "I Can Only Imagine."

"When you lie down"

Bedtime is one of the easiest times to teach our children, through Bible stories and prayers. When they're young, we may teach prayers they can memorize and recite. Then, as they get older, we teach them to pray about their needs and for others. We teach them to ask for God's forgiveness if they've misbehaved.

"When you rise up"

Teaching when we rise up in the morning is also an easily established routine. I've already mentioned how I would take Lauren from her crib to the window and say, "Thank You, God, for this beautiful day." It taught her to think of God when she first wakes and to give thanks to the God who made this day, the earth and sky.

As I've said, breakfast is an easy way to feed your children spiritually while you feed them physically. We would often focus on one verse, discuss its meaning, and use that as our memory verse. Using the *Kidz Time 1: Bible Verses A to Z* was fun. Then, on the way to school, I'd call out "A!" and the kids would reply, "All we like sheep have gone astray!" "B!" I'd continue. "But the very hairs of your head are numbered." We sometimes posted verses on the bathroom mirror so the children could be reminded of them while brushing their teeth or combing their hair.

Plan A Mom Tip

Defuse the land mine of neglecting to teach your children God's Word by teaching them today.

Moms, today you have so many resources. Don't fall for Satan's lie that teaching your kids is cumbersome or that you don't have time. What are you waiting for? You may not have tomorrow.

Live Out Loud

Plan A Mom Checkup

1. What has been my excuse or reason for not daily teaching my children?
2. The following best describes me:
   - ☐ I don't daily teach my children about God.
   - ☐ I teach my children about God sometimes.
   - ☐ I diligently teach my children about God.

Love Out Loud

1. Do you think it's more common to diligently teach one's children about God or leave it up to someone else?
2. How do James 4:13–14 and 1 Peter 2:9 speak to your responsibility to diligently teach your children?
3. What did you learn about the importance of your heart being filled with God's Word so you can teach your children? How do you fill your heart?
4. What impact does Kamal Saleem's mother's diligent teaching have on you?
5. How and when do you plan to implement diligently teaching God's Word to your children?

Between You and God—Principle to Remember

I defuse the land mine of procrastination
by teaching my children about God today.

Father, thank You for giving me the privilege of teaching my children about You. Help me be sensitive to Your leading and how to teach them. Help them to receive Your teachings with open, responsive hearts. In Jesus' name, amen.

Laugh Out Loud

When Rachel was three, I couldn't find her in the house one day. I panicked! Finally, I found her in my closet, behind some boxes, eating a lollipop. "Rachel, what are you doing in there?" I asked.

"Hiiiiiding," she replied slowly. "Why?" I probed. "Because I thought what I was doing wouldn't make you very happy."

It seemed young for a child to learn about her conscience and the Holy Spirit, but it was the sweetest and most perfect teachable moment I have experienced in motherhood.—Charla Simpson

STUCK IN SINGLE-MOM GRIEF OR RESPONDING TO GOD'S VOICE

I defuse the land mine of being stuck in grief
by responding to the voice of God.

*"God heard the lad crying; and the angel of God
called to Hagar from heaven."*

Genesis 21:17

"What would you say is the number-one emotion a mother has when her husband leaves her for another woman or says he doesn't love her any more, or when she finds out he's been lying to her and is having an affair?" I asked.

Here are the responses I received:

"Pain, fear, and betrayal, which all lead to a LOT OF ANGER."

"Shock, anger, betrayal, rejection, and sadness all at the same time. Also goes for when you get left for a man."

"The number-one emotion I felt when my husband of twenty-five years told me of his affairs was, 'What??' It was a complete betrayal of my innocence and trust. There is not a word that can describe such an emotion, because there's such a mixture of anger, love, fear, and anxiety. Those were years of survival, when our great God kept after me to trust Him, knowing 'trust' was a dirty word for me. But God has proved

to be faithful even in my anger and all the other emotions I felt, even when I failed miserably to even muster up a mustard seed of faith."

"Teaching others to trust when trust has been violated is impossible. But not with the God of all hope, who continues to reach my heart with His faithfulness, care, protection, and unconditional love. Is there a human man out there like that? Introduce me! He will have to measure up to my heavenly Father."

"For me, anger. My first husband abused me verbally and physically for about six months before I left him. Our children were two years old and five months old. I actually found out about his affair after I left, and was very angry. I know God had greater plans for me, but at the time it was really hard. I had to be on guard because I had two girls and was single. I started back to church. Satan tried to sway me, but I had friends who helped. My ex continued to come to my apartment and try to work things out. I'd struggled for two years before I left him. The divorce was bad, and I wanted to make the marriage work, but in the five months between leaving and filing for divorce, he continued to abuse me. I had to make sure that my girls didn't get hurt in that or any future relationships I had. It was better to go through the divorce and be single with two children. I was twenty-one. God brought me another husband who adopted my girls, yet it's been a difficult journey with one daughter in particular because she never sees her real father."

"I went through denial for a long time, then hurt and wondering, if I had done things differently, would he still be here? 'What did I do wrong? What does he see in her that he doesn't see in me?' kept running through my head. But then I looked at my little boy (Eli was almost two) and realized I had raised him by myself since the day he was born, and someone—me—had to keep taking care of him. My ex would not help at all. He refused to feed Eli, change him, bathe him, etc. I would make him feed him a bottle every once in a while just to try and get them to bond.

Being a single mom is extremely difficult, but I think it made me strong. My number-one strength is adaptability. I'm not afraid of much because I look at what I've been through and realize I can do anything. I've relied a lot on my parents and Jesus, and I've gotten really close to feeling like I can't make it, but I've survived."

"Coming out of a bad relationship, you often wish children weren't involved. There were days when I didn't want to get out of bed or even move due to depression and the flood of emotions. But knowing I had to take care of the children made me get up and move. That doesn't mean when the kids are in bed you don't just lose it. You have to realize that it is a normal process, and it takes time to heal. I found keeping busy and shopping (Grandma said shopping always makes you feel better)—not necessarily buying anything, but getting out—helped a lot.

You have to try to find the good in the situation, which can be hard. The best thing that came out of my situation was my child. Also, I was one who only believed in getting married once. But I also don't believe God meant for you to be miserable for the rest of your life. What I mean by that is, after my husband cheated on me with multiple girls, multiple times, I decided I needed to be closer to family, so I moved. I had several family members and friends who thought I should try to work it out; but if the spouse doesn't want to be with you, you can't make him."

"I followed God's Word in my heart, even in my actions. I was celibate before marriage. Now my husband is possibly going to jail for five years for sexual assault. I have been told that I am strong. In spite of my strength, I don't believe I can raise our children. I know God is with me, but I am imperfect. I don't want to fail these wonderful babies. Why, God? I don't understand why!"

Pam Kanaly, cofounder of Survive 'N' Thrive, a national conference for single mothers, also speaks from experience. "Every single mom's story initially begins at the same place: grief. However, it's important to understand that grief is a necessary part of healing. It allows one to face the sadness and destruction of a dream. To not grieve would be to 'stuff,' which is destructive.

"There comes a time when every single mother needs to make a deliberate choice to redefine her family. She does that by purposefully seeking God's voice and plans. Though loneliness and loss plague single moms through every stage of the healing process, it's possible through Christ to settle into a mode of inner contentment; one in which she finally embraces Jesus as her 'husband,' releases the grip of anger, and rejects the false notion that she'll never have a fulfilling life unless God brings her another husband to complete her family."

Hope for the Plan B Single Mom

As you can see, and as many of you know firsthand, single-mom emotions run the gamut from the deepest grief to peaks of anger. It's normal to question and ask why—realizing, however, that there may never be a satisfactory answer. God's Plan A is for us to love Him with all our heart, soul, and mind and be united with a man who loves God with all his heart, soul, and mind. God's Plan A is for us not only to love Him in that manner, but also to love our spouse as we love ourselves. Anything less falls into Plan B.

In preparing for this chapter, I searched for a woman in the Bible who was divorced and raised her child alone. I thought of numerous widows. I thought of Eunice, who was married but not to a Christian. I did a search for a divorced woman raising a child by herself. I couldn't find even one . . . until God led me to Genesis 21:10–21.

Genesis 21 is predominantly about the birth of Isaac, long awaited-child promised to Abram and Sarai. But it's also about a divorced, single mom.

As we've already seen, ten years before Isaac was born, Sarai had become impatient with her barrenness. Convinced that she and Abram weren't going to have the Plan A child God had promised, she took things into her own hands. You'll recall, she gave her maid Hagar to her husband as "his wife" (Genesis 16:3).

But Sarai was wrong, and after much upheaval (and under new, God-given names), Sarah and Abraham did have the promised child. At the feast celebrating Isaac's being weaned, Sarah saw Ishmael, Hagar's son, mocking Isaac. This didn't set well with Sarah, and she demanded of Abraham, "Drive out *this maid* and *her* son, for the son of *this maid* shall not be an heir with my son Isaac. The matter distressed Abraham greatly because of *his* son. But God said to Abraham, 'Do not be distressed because of the lad and *your maid*; whatever Sarah tells you, listen to her, for through Isaac your descendants shall be named. And of the son of the maid I will make a nation also, because he is your descendant. So Abraham rose early in the morning and took bread and a skin of water and gave them to Hagar, putting them on her shoulder, and *gave her the boy, and sent her away*. And she departed and wandered about in the wilderness of Beersheba" (Genesis 21:10–14, italics mine).

If ever there was an account of a divorce, I think we just read it. Hagar has gone from being Sarah's maid to Abraham's wife to "this maid" to God referring to her as Abraham's maid. Abraham is "greatly distressed" because of Ishmael, "his son." Imagine the pain in his heart when the son he had raised for ten years and whom he thought was God's promised heir was given to Hagar. The Bible tells us Abraham put bread and a skin of water on Hagar's shoulder, but he put more than that on her shoulders when he sent her away. He put the burden of surviving and raising their son by herself.

But keep reading. Genesis 21:15–21 is the first of many accounts of God's faithfulness to single moms and their children. After Hagar had wandered in the wilderness and the water in the skin was gone, the Bible tells us she left Ishmael under a bush. "Then she went and sat down opposite him, about a bowshot away, for she said, 'Do not let me see the boy die.' And she sat opposite him, and lifted up her voice and wept" (Genesis 21:15–16). We can only imagine the intensity of grief and despair that both Hagar and Ishmael felt as they wandered, parched, knowing that back home others were feasting with drinks, fruits, cheeses, breads, and meats. What anger must have swelled in Hagar. Surely she railed, "I didn't ask for any of this!" What went on in Ishmael's mind? Was he stunned and mystified? "All this just because I made fun of my half brother?"

Plan Bs often stink. In the midst of them, we may have more questions than answers. We may feel like Hagar, lifting up our voice weeping.

But Hagar wasn't the only one crying. Genesis 21:17 says, "God heard the lad crying." Moms, I pray it encourages you to know that God heard Ishmael crying. The Scriptures are written to encourage us. You may feel you can't take another day; that you're not going to make it. You may be grieving because you don't see a way out of your problems or you don't know how to help your child. When you feel that way, remember that God heard Ishmael crying. He saw Hagar. Not only did God hear and see them, He called to them from heaven: "'What is the matter with you, Hagar? Do not fear, for God has heard the voice of the lad where he is. Arise, lift up the lad, and hold him by the hand, for I will make a great nation of him.' Then God opened her eyes and she saw a well of water; and she went and filled the skin with water and gave the lad a drink. God was with the lad, and he grew; and he lived in the wilderness and became an archer. He lived in the wilderness of Paran, and his mother took a wife for him from the land of Egypt" (Genesis 21:17–21).

Plan B Truths to Remember

This story gives us several important points to remember when we're in the wilderness of Plan B:

- Although you have a weight of responsibility on your shoulders, you're not alone.
- God hears you and your child crying.
- God sees you and your child. He knows where you and your child are.
- The Lord calls to you from heaven.
- God wants to open your eyes to His provisions, hope, and opportunities.
- God calls you to take what is in your hand, fill it with His provision, and give it to your children.

Stuck in Grief or Responding to God's Voice

Hagar paid attention when God spoke to her. That's our responsibility also. We can't see down the road or what's going to happen to our children or us. However, we can rest assured that wherever we are, God is a present help in time of need.

Plan A Mom Tip

Defuse the land mine of being stuck in grief by recognizing God's presence and responding to His help.

Our story concludes with the following information: God was with Ishmael, who lived and grew, became an archer, and married (Genesis 21:20–21). And we know he had children: Muslims claim Abraham as their father through Ishmael. In spite of some troubled times in his youth, this man lived and prospered because God was looking out for him, and because his mother responded to God's voice.

LIVE OUT LOUD

Plan A Mom Checkup

1. Am I stuck in grief, anger, and denial? (Although grieving is necessary and an important part of the healing process, recognize that God doesn't want you to sit there and die any more than He wanted that for Hagar and her son.)

2. In the midst of raising my children, am I crying out to God or just trying to forge ahead on my own?

3. After I lift up my voice to God, do I pay attention to what He says to me? Do I have my Bible open so I can go to scriptures He directs me to? Do I keep a journal and pen handy so I can write down what He impresses on my heart?

4. When God directs me, do I get up and do what He shows or tells me?

5. Is my life a witness that, although I may have been treated badly by another person, God is watching out for my children and me?

6. Am I continuing to walk faithfully before God so my children benefit from the overflow of God's provision in my life?

7. Do I daily replenish my heart at the wellspring of the Holy Spirit?

8. Do I point my children to the source of Living Water so they can be filled and live by God's provision and for His glory?

LOVE OUT LOUD

1. What have you learned from the account of Sarah, Abraham, Isaac, Hagar, and Ishmael?

2. Why are John 8:37–39 and Ephesians 5:18 important if you want to hear God's voice and receive His help?

3. What message does God have for you to share with a single mom who may be grieving a spouse's death or divorce?

4. What could you teach your children about God's concern for them based on this passage?

5. Which of the verses do you want to memorize? Why?

Between You and God—Principle to Remember

I defuse the land mine of being
stuck in grief by responding to God's voice.

Father, thank You that You see my children and me. Thank You for hearing when we call to You. Thank You for Your provisions. Help me be more sensitive to Your voice and quick to obey. Fill me from the wellspring of Your Holy Spirit. Let your Living Water gurgle up inside of me and overflow to my children. Teach them to call out and listen to You. In Jesus' name, amen.

Laugh Out Loud

When the kids were little, and right after my good friend Debra passed away, they were asking lots of questions, like, "Can Aunt Debra fly?" "Can Aunt Debra see us?" I was still really sad and didn't want to talk about it much. Finally, I said, "We know Aunt Debra is in heaven with Jesus and isn't sick anymore. That's really all we know." To this Daniel replied, "Mom, we know one more thing about Aunt Debra. We know everyone clapped when she walked into heaven." I asked him how we know that, and he said, "Isn't that what the applause of heaven means?" I'd been reading a book by that title, and Daniel put it together. I like to think he's right.—Pam Couch

PRODIGAL-CHILD DESPAIR OR FAITHFUL INTERCESSION

I defuse the land mine of despair by
faithfully interceding for my prodigal.

*O Lord, the God of my salvation, I have cried out by day and in the night
before You. Let my prayer come before You; incline Your ear to my cry!*

Psalm 88:1–2

"I don't know where my son is. I haven't seen or talked to him in fourteen years."

Staring at the mother seated next to me, my heart melted as I tried to imagine what it would be like to not have talked to Taylor or known where he was for fourteen years. Even now the thought makes my eyes well up with tears. Other moms suffer the grief of *knowing* where their child is: sleeping under a bridge, at a halfway house, working as a stripper at a nightclub, behind prison bars, running from the law. Or, sometimes, the prodigal is working at a great job and happily married but has turned his or her back on the Lord.

The word *prodigal* comes from the Latin *prodigus*, from *prodigere*: to drive away, squander. It means recklessly extravagant, characterized by wasteful expenditure.[1] Never is it a Plan A mom's wish that her child become a prodigal.

In Christian circles, when we think of a prodigal, we most often think of the prodigal son in Jesus' parable, recorded in Luke 15:11–32. In this story a son takes his share of his father's fortune and squanders it in reckless living. Finally, when he hits bottom, he returns to his father and begs for forgiveness. The father graciously embraces and forgives his son—a poignant analogy of sinners repenting and returning to God.

In this parable the obvious stands out: the prodigal squandered his financial inheritance and lived an immoral lifestyle. For purposes of this chapter, however, I believe God would have us also recognize the danger of squandering one's spiritual inheritance. Some children raised in Christian homes squander the riches of Bible teaching and godly upbringing they received. Certainly, God's heart aches for both the child who is squandering his life in immoral living and the child who is living a moral life but squandering his spiritual inheritance.

If you have a prodigal who is wasting that which was entrusted to him or her, take heart. There's hope. We see that in Jochebed and her children.

Lessons from Jochebed

The midwife handed Jochebed her baby. Before she even looked between his wiggly legs, she already knew by the midwife's expression that it was a boy. Tears welled in Jochebed's eyes as she clutched Moses to her breast. "I won't give him up!" Jochebed announced in defiance of Pharaoh's law that every Hebrew male infant be put to death. Tears streaming down her face, she said again, softly: "I won't give him up." Looking deeply into her son's eyes for the first time, her expression changed. He was beautiful. There was something extraordinary about him. At that moment Jochebed resolved to do everything possible to save her son's life. "God has a plan for your life, little one," she whispered as he nursed peacefully, innocent of the danger surrounding him or the adventuresome life he would lead.

I doubt there's a mother reading this book who isn't familiar with the story of Moses and how he delivered the Hebrew people from Egyptian bondage. But if we rewind Moses' life to his first forty years, we can take a look at his life from his mother's perspective.

Jochebed's Perspective

Jochebed held a beautiful baby boy in her arms. The Hebrew word translated "beautiful" in Exodus 2:2 signifies more than handsome. It carries with it the concept of "good" and "excellent." In the apostle Stephen's inspired sermon in Acts 7:20, he used the words "lovely in the sight of God" to describe what Jochebed saw in Moses. Herbert Lockyer, in *All the Women of the Bible*, writes, "There was something other-worldly or angelic about his features. As the little one lay in her lap, Jochebed felt that he had been sent from God, and that He, along with her mingled faith and love, would somehow preserve the child."[2]

Jochebed's Plans

Jochebed devised a plan to save Moses' life. Against all odds, she hid him for three months from the Egyptians. Did she babysit an infant girl and send her older daughter, Miriam, out of the house with Moses when authorities searched for a crying child? We don't know. But we do know she was a woman who planned, who fought for her child to protect him from the evil of the day.

Not only did Jochebed plan to hide Moses—and succeed in this for three months—but she also planned for the next stage of his life, when she could no longer conceal him. How did she conceive the idea of a floating cradle? I think she was divinely inspired. Instead of letting things happen to her son, this mother took proactive steps to protect him. She looked around her. She paid attention. She listened. She heard that Pharaoh's daughter was softhearted. She found out where this woman bathed. She prayed. She knew the dangers of the Nile River, yet rather than allow ruthless Egyptians to throw Moses into the waters, she strategically placed him where he had a chance of survival. While other mothers were wringing their hands, she wove a basket of reeds.

Jochebed's Prayer

I've seen a bumper sticker that reads, "As long as there are tests in school, there will be prayer." Although Exodus 2:3 doesn't explicitly state, "Then Jochebed prayed," I can't imagine her not praying as she covered the wicker basket with tar and pitch, gently placed her beloved Moses inside, and set the cradle among the reeds by the bank of the Nile. I can't imagine the grief and anxiety of placing my infant into a basket and leaving him. Of course, she didn't leave her babe unguarded. She stationed Miriam, her older daughter, at a distance to watch and see what became of Moses. When Pharaoh's daughter came to bathe, she saw the basket and had pity on Moses, who was crying. Clever Miriam suddenly appears by her side and offers to find a Hebrew woman to nurse Moses. "Go ahead," Pharaoh's daughter agrees, surely realizing exactly the scheme in which she was participating.

Jochebed's Prize

Imagine what it must have been like when Pharaoh's daughter, beautifully made up and royally dressed, looked into the eyes of the Hebrew slave who was, no doubt, trying to hold back her tears. Never did a mother hear more precious words than those Pharaoh's daughter spoke: "Take this child away and nurse him for me and I shall give you your wages" (Exodus 2:9). How did Jochebed contain herself from jumping with joy, from smothering her baby boy with kisses as she praised God for not only sparing her son's life but also providing wages while she nursed and raised her tiny tike for three years!

Jochebed's Purpose

At some point in our parenting, we may question our purpose in life. How well Jochebed points us to that purpose: to give and preserve life; to prepare our children to fulfill God's purposes for their lives.

Exodus 2:10 says succinctly, "The child grew, and she [Jochebed] brought him to Pharaoh's daughter and he became her son." This is the second time Jochebed has had to say good-bye to her son. Which was harder—when he was three months or three years old, reaching out and crying for his mommy as a stranger led him away to the strange palace?

Even in the short time Jochebed had with her son, she fulfilled her purpose in Moses' life. She saved her infant son from death and prepared him for his future by planting spiritual truths, songs, and his Hebrew heritage in his heart. Those seeds took root. When Moses was forty, he sided with his people.

Sadly, he did it in a way that set him on a course that would have brought heartache to Jochebed. He murdered an Egyptian who was beating a Hebrew slave, then hid the dead man in the sand. If we could go back in time and freeze the moment when Jochebed heard that Moses had murdered someone, we would have most likely seen her shock and despair as she wondered, "How could my son have done such a thing?"

When Jochebed received news that Pharaoh was again trying to kill Moses, can you imagine the thoughts and emotions that surged through her? Then Jochebed got word that Moses had fled to the desert. Moses, the one who had been spared, the one with a rich Jewish heritage, the one educated by the finest of Egyptian teachers—at age forty a fugitive, a man without a country, a prodigal who appears to have just wasted his opportunities in life, squandering his rich inheritance.

Hope for Your Prodigal

Janet Thompson, speaker and author of *Praying for Your Prodigal Daughter*, shares insights for moms who may relate to Jochebed; who may be wondering where their child is and are praying their prodigal is restored to God and them.

"Congratulations! You're pregnant!" Many of us responded in awe and exhilarated anticipation of the precious gift God was giving us. We had great plans and expectations for the bundle of joy that would soon be placed in our arms. I don't think anyone looks into baby blue eyes and thinks: "Now, this child is going to be a prodigal." I know I didn't.

Abandoning the dreams and plans we had for our son or daughter, surrendering our Plan A to an unknown and precarious Plan B, may be the hardest point for any parent to reach. I know parents who dreamed of helping their daughter plan a lavish wedding only to hurriedly throw together a simple ceremony because she was pregnant. Or they'd dreamed of being by their daughter's side when she delivered her first baby but learn that she gave away a child or maybe had an abortion. The son with a bright future as a lawyer ends up serving time in jail instead. The list goes on. Each of us with a prodigal child has our own story of heartache and loss.

When my daughter, Kim, went to her dad's and my alma mater, I wanted her to experience the same college dorm life and campus activities I had enjoyed, but I realized that was my dream for her. I had to relinquish it to the choices she was making for her college life—living with her boyfriend. I pulled out all the stops trying to dissuade her, but my pleading and warnings fell on deaf ears. She was determined to do college her way.

Even though I cringed every time I had to explain her living situation to others and became defensive if any of my friends said anything judgmental, I had to continually ask myself whether I was more worried about what they thought of her or what they thought of me.

Life isn't fair, and the Bible never promises that it will be. Though we strive to lead a good life, there's no guarantee that things will always go our way. But what the Bible does say is that instead of grumbling about our circumstances, we should embrace them as an opportunity for growth. James 1:2–3 puts it this way: "Dear brothers and sisters, when troubles come your way, consider it an opportunity for great joy. For you know that when your faith is tested, your endurance has a chance to grow" (NLT).

This is a difficult verse to accept. I don't want to rejoice in my troubles, I want to wallow in them. I wish my faith didn't have to endure hardships—like dealing with a prodigal daughter. But if we focus on God's plan and purpose instead of how our prodigal situation impacts us, our prayers will be more effective as we align ourselves with His plan for our child and for us. I know this might seem harsh, but sometimes we need a reminder that, hey—this isn't about us. Our child is making choices we can't control. That's humbling. Up to this point, he or she has been in our "protective custody." It strikes a blow to our egos that now our kids think they can make their own decisions, and we are powerless to stop them from making bad ones.

It hurts to admit that we can no longer protect them from harm. It's what we've done their entire life, and now they're trying to take that role away from us. Peace comes when we finally realize that we'll do what we can, but we have to let God be God. He's omnipotent; we're not. Only God can protect our child and help him or her make the right decisions. This isn't admitting defeat—it's admitting we cannot do this alone. We need God. Our child needs prayer.

You may have heard the phrase "Let go and let God." In fact, that's what some may have counseled you, and you wondered, "Let God do what?" It simply means we are to fully and completely put our hope and trust in the Lord and His plan for our prodigal child as we continue reading and praying His Word and His promises. Even though our child may be out of our sight, he or she is never out of God's sight. God is omnipresent—something we could never be. Like us, He's shedding tears for our child, but He's also battling Satan for that child's life. Our part in the battle is to pray. When my daughter, Kim, was far from God, I continually prayed that He would surround her with Christians everywhere she turned.

If we don't see our prodigal child return, we wonder, "Wasn't God listening?" Did He turn a deaf ear to our prayers? Why didn't He bring him or her back? These *are all legitimate questions—and hard ones not to have answered. Many things in life will be beyond our understanding until we get to heaven. Maybe our child accepted Jesus but walked away and has led a terrible, miserable life on earth. God still welcomes believers home: "God so loved our child that he gave his one and only Son, so that if he or she believes in him they will not perish but have eternal life" (personalized from John 3:16). The enemy can steal earthly joy and peace, but he can't steal salvation, because "the one who is in our child is greater than the one who is in the world" (personalized from 1 John 4:4). This is the hope and faith that gives us peace.*

Don't give up. Don't stop praying. Do allow yourself to grieve and mourn for the loss of your child or the vision you had for him or her. Then trust God and wait for Him to work.

Faithful waiting means entrusting our children to God and faithfully praying with the expectation of the goodness of God's sovereign plan in His perfect timing. God can turn any Plan B back to His Plan A. And so we pray for God's will, and we wait for His answer.

After persistently praying God's Word and will for my daughter daily for five years, she left her boyfriend and returned home. With renewed hope, I continued praying that she also would return to God. One year later she met her future husband, who was not a believer. While I questioned God's plan, I continued praying expectantly. God answered my prayers beyond my wildest dreams. Kim and her fiancé, Toby, accepted Christ in a biblically based premarital course my husband and I gave them as an engagement gift. Today they are raising their three children in a Christ-centered home. Keep praying![β]

We don't know if Jochebed was still alive when Moses, at eighty years of age, returned to Egypt. However, we know the unmistakable impact his mother made on his early years. No doubt she whispered to him many times, "God has a special plan for your life. God miraculously spared you. He's going to use you one day for His purposes." I believe Jochebed planted those truths in Moses' heart and he never forgot them. We, like Jochebed, can plant the same truths in our children's hearts no matter how old they are.

Jochebed's prodigal returned and fulfilled God's plans for his life. Janet's prodigal also returned. One of the things Janet mentioned doing was praying the Scriptures for her daughter. To pray the Scriptures means to pray Bible verses for your child. This is good to do whether your child is a prodigal or walking with God. Just this morning, as I read 1 Thessalonians 5:13–24, God moved me to pray those verses for my children. How did I pray them? By interjecting or substituting personalizations, where appropriate, to the passage. Following is my personalized scripture prayer, with my words set in boldface type:

> *"**Father**, encourage **Taylor, Ali, Lauren, and Chris today**. Help **them be strong and** patient with everyone. See that no one repays another with evil for evil, but **help them** always seek after that which is good for one another and for all people. **Help them** rejoice always; pray without ceasing; **and** in everything give thanks; for this is **Your** will for **them** in Christ Jesus. **Help them** not **to** quench the Spirit **or** despise prophetic utterances. **Help them to** examine everything carefully; hold fast to that which is good; **and** abstain from every form of evil. God of peace, sanctify **them** entirely; and may **their** spirit and soul and body be preserved complete, without blame at the coming of our Lord Jesus Christ. **God, You have been** faithful to call **them**, and **You** also will bring it to pass. **Thank You for bringing this to pass.**"*

Plan A Mom Tip

Tell your children often that God has a plan for their life. Daily plant God's Word in their minds so it can take root in their hearts. Never give up. Never quit praying for your children.

When we pray the Scriptures for our children, we have confidence that we're praying in accordance with God's will and what He wants for our children. By praying different verses for our children day by day, we are being proactive in their lives. You may choose to read a verse or several and pray those during your devotional time with your children. Or, if they've left home, you may pray them in your personal devotional time. Either way, you can be assured God hears your prayers.

LIVE OUT LOUD

Plan A Mom Checkup

1. Do I have a vision for my child, knowing that God has a plan for his or her life?
2. When and how do I do to instill that vision in my child?
3. When the vision doesn't seem to be coming to pass—when it appears my children are squandering that which has been entrusted to them—do I give up in despair? Or do I hold to the knowledge that God wants to use them? Do I continue to intercede for my children and encourage them?
4. Try praying one or several of the following scriptures for your child.

• Matthew 6:13	• Mark 12:22
• Luke 4:12	• John 17:15, 17
• Acts 1:8; 3:39	• Romans 12:1–2
• 1 Corinthians 6:18–20	• 2 Corinthians 2:15
• Galatians 5:16	• Ephesians 4:23–5:21
• Colossians 3:1–2	• 1 Thessalonians 5:8–9, 19
• 2 Thessalonians 3:3	• 1 Timothy 4:8–9
• 2 Timothy 1:6; 2:21–22	• Titus 2:11; 3:14
• Philemon 1:25	• Hebrews 2:18, 12:1, 28
• James 1:16; 4:7–8, 10	• 1 Peter 1:15; 2:25; 3:15; 4:2; 5:6–9
• 2 Peter 1:5–7	• 1 John 1:9; 3:7–8; 4:1–3
• 2 John 1:6	• 3 John 1:2
• Jude 1:21–21, 24	• Revelation 3:19–22; 22:7

LOVE OUT LOUD

1. Which do you think is worse: to squander one's financial or spiritual entrustment?

2. What encourages you from Janet's testimony of her experience with her prodigal?

3. What do you learn from Jochebed?

4. Which of the following best describes your thoughts?

    ☐ I don't pray all that much because I expect my little one to grow up and be just fine.

    ☐ I pray purposefully and pray the Scriptures for my child, realizing that evil and temptations of the flesh are part of the world in which we live.

5. Which Bible verse(s) from the Live Out Loud section, question 4, did you pray for your children? What benefits of praying scriptures are there for you and your child?

BETWEEN YOU AND GOD—PRINCIPLE TO REMEMBER

I defuse the land mine of despair by faithfully interceding for my prodigal.

Father, thank You that You know where my child is physically and spiritually. Thank You for Your presence with them. Help them to turn away from the vain things of the world and turn to serve You. In Jesus' name, amen.

LAUGH OUT LOUD

Hannah was playing in her room when she slipped and hit her ear on her toy box. It wouldn't stop bleeding, so we took her to the emergency room, and she had surgery. I didn't get a clear explanation of what had happened until about a month later. She then told me the story, adding: "If a trampoline had been there (pointing to the spot where she slipped) I would have been fine!"—Amber Davis

10

MOTHER KNOWS BEST OR GOD KNOWS BEST

I defuse the land mine of thinking I know what's best for my
children by trusting that God's ways are higher than my ways.

*As the heavens are higher than the earth, so are My ways higher
than your ways and My thoughts than your thoughts.*

Isaiah 55:9

From the moment I found out I was pregnant, I scoured books to find out
what was best for the precious little one growing inside of me. Determined that
nothing would go into my mouth and his developing body that was bad for him, I
eliminated coffee, soft drinks, and diet products. I ate healthy, whole foods because
I wanted to give Taylor every possible benefit of a well-developed body and mind.
I did the same with Lauren. People prodded me, "Oh, that piece of cake won't hurt
you, nor will those chips, French fries, or a few cups of this or that." However, "this
and that" didn't provide my baby with God's wholesome foods. They were processed,
full of chemicals or sugar, and of little nutritional benefit. I knew what was best for
my unborn babies and did my best to choose the best for them.

When Taylor and Lauren were born, I continued to study and tried to choose
for them what I considered best. I read that breast milk was best, which fit with my
desire to nurse my babies. When they grew to an age where they could be weaned, I

studied what foods were best for their growing bodies and chose those. Cookies and sugar didn't touch my little ones' lips until their one-year birthday, when they got their first taste of birthday cake.

As Taylor and Lauren grew, I assumed responsibility for not only what went in their bodies but also their minds and spirits. Some people laughed at me for not allowing them to watch certain television shows or movies. But in my heart, I knew it was my responsibility to choose only that which was best for them to see or hear and to protect their innocence as long as possible from that which wasn't edifying. I knew it was best to protect their pure hearts and minds from violence, course-talking characters, sex scenes, and dark themes, and I stuck to my convictions. I offered alternate programs at home and took videos to others' homes where my kids were being babysat.

Keith and I tried to do what was best for our children in regard not only to what they took in but also what they gave out. We taught them the "magic words" *please* and *thank you* and to say "Yes, sir" or "No, ma'am."

Even if your rules are different from mine, I have no doubt you also did—and continue to do—what you consider best for your children. The television show *Father Knows Best* might easily had a sister program *Mother Knows Best*—the point being that parents have a leg up on kids in knowing what's good for them. I think that's why it's so hard when the time arrives in our child's life when we can no longer enforce adherence to what we consider best for them. The Plan B may come through an illness, a learning disability, an accident in which they are involved—or, when they're adults, job loss, marital problems, infertility, or any other number of things.

A Promising Beginning

Our Plan A for our children will not always turn out. Even though we raise them the "best" we can, they have their own plans for their lives—as does God. Part of parenting is learning when to let go and trust God, understanding that His ways are higher and better than ours, even though we can't see it at the time.

John the Baptist's mother, Elizabeth, is an example to us of a mom who probably thought she knew what was best for her son but had to come to grips with the truth that God knows best.

Both she and her husband, Zacharias, raised John the best they could. Zacharias was a priest, and Elizabeth was a descendent of Aaron, the first high priest and father of the priestly line. This power couple is identified in Luke 1:6 as "righteous in the sight of God, walking blamelessly in all the commandments and requirements of the Lord." However, Luke 1:7 announces the Plan B in their lives: "They had no child, because Elizabeth was barren, and they were advanced in years." There it is. There's no perfect couple, situation, or life. You may do all you can to be the perfect person, and things still won't work out perfectly.

In the course of Zacharias's faithful performance of his priestly office, he was chosen to enter the temple to burn incense before the Lord. Following is the exciting account of what happened.

The whole multitude of the people were in prayer outside at the hour of the incense offering. And an angel of the Lord appeared to him, standing to the right of the altar of incense. Zacharias was troubled when he saw the angel, and fear gripped him. But the angel said to him, "Do not be afraid, Zacharias, for your petition has been heard, and your wife Elizabeth will bear you a son, and you will give him the name John. "You will have joy and gladness, and many will rejoice at his birth. For he will be great in the sight of the Lord; and he will drink no wine or liquor, and he will be filled with the Holy Spirit while yet in his mother's womb. And he will turn many of the sons of Israel back to the Lord their God. It is he who will go as a forerunner before Him in the spirit and power of Elijah, to turn the hearts of the fathers back to the children, and the disobedient to the attitude of the righteous, so as to make ready a people prepared for the Lord."

Zacharias said to the angel, "How will I know this for certain? For I am an old man and my wife is advanced in years."

The angel answered and said to him, "I am Gabriel, who stands in the presence of God, and I have been sent to speak to you and to bring you this good news. And behold, you shall be silent and unable to speak until the day when these things take place, because you did not believe my words, which will be fulfilled in their proper time."

The people were waiting for Zacharias, and were wondering at his delay in the temple. But when he came out, he was unable to speak to them; and they realized he had seen a vision in the temple; and he kept making signs to them, and remained mute. When the days of his priestly service were ended, he went back home. After these days Elizabeth his wife became pregnant, and she kept herself in seclusion for five months, saying, "This is the way the Lord has dealt with me in the days when He looked with favor upon me, to take away my disgrace among men" (Luke 1:10–25).

If ever there were a happy announcement about the arrival of a baby, this is it. No sonogram was necessary. Straight from heaven, Gabriel, an angelic messenger, gives Zacharias and Elizabeth the best news they could receive. Not only were they going to have a baby in their old age, a miracle in itself, but their little one was going to bring them joy and gladness. While Elizabeth's baby was still in her womb, God would fill him with His Spirit. John would drink no wine or liquor. God's calling on John would be to turn many people back to the Lord. The angel announced to Zacharias that their son would be a forerunner of the Messiah and would go before Him in the spirit and power of Elijah. What better words could have fallen on a parent's ears?

Though Zacharias initially doubted, Elizabeth immediately believed. And when she was in her sixth month, Gabriel paid another visit to earth, this time to a young virgin named Mary in Nazareth. You know the story. After conceiving Christ by the Holy Spirit, Mary went to visit her Aunt Elizabeth. The moment Elizabeth heard Mary's voice, John leaped in her womb. Both women were elated. They could not contain their joy at God's choosing them. Their children would be the greatest of the great—chosen, selected by God—one the Messiah and one who would prepare the way for Him.

If only we could capture that moment when the two women embraced and were filled with the Spirit, and the babies within them were filled with the Holy Spirit. I wonder what they talked about over the months of Mary's extended visit. I imagine Zacharias joined in as they pored over the Law and the Prophets, seeking to better understand God's role for their unborn sons.

Mom's Plan versus God's Plan

What I would give to know a few of the daily details of John's upbringing. His saintly, elderly parents likely had their hands full. What transpired in those years between John's eighth-day circumcision and his adult life as indicated in Luke 1:80 ("The child continued to grow and to become strong in spirit, and he lived in the deserts until the day of his public appearance to Israel")? How many times did Elizabeth have to call John in from chasing lizards to sit down for his Scripture lessons? Did she ever wonder how God would use him if he couldn't learn to speak in a quieter, more respectful tone of voice? Did she pull her hair out in frustration at his strong will and grow exasperated telling him to take off those animal skins and put on some normal clothes? When she saw him pick up and nibble his first locust, did she scream, "Get that out of your mouth!"? Did Elizabeth continually repeat to herself that God had a plan for her son's life and that she'd just have to trust Him? I think the answer is probably yes.

What did Elizabeth think when, instead of following in Zacharias's footsteps and serving in the temple, John turned his back and headed for the desert? Did she try to reason with her son? "Gabriel said you're going to be the Messiah's forerunner. How can you be His forerunner if you're off who knows where?" Certainly this godly mother knew what was best for her son. Or did she?

John didn't follow traditional religion in the sense of worship method and dress code. His ministry was not in the synagogue but in the wilderness and around the Jordon River. John didn't follow traditional teaching of laws and rules either; he preached a baptism of repentance for the forgiveness of sins (Luke 3:2–3). He didn't tell those who came to hear him preach how wonderful they were; he called out their hypocrisy and told them to bear fruit in keeping with repentance (Luke 3:7–8). John preached a baptism of the Holy Spirit and fire, which comes from Jesus (Luke 3:16). He preached judgment and the gospel (Luke 3:17–18). He got in political leader's faces and confronted their sin (Luke 3:19). And he suffered for his righteousness stand: Herod threw him in prison (Luke 3:21).

Where was Elizabeth during all this? Was she already in her grave? Was she alive and fretting, wondering what had become of her son? Was she cheering him on . . . until he landed in jail? Was she crying out to God, "What happened to the joy and gladness you promised? What's my son doing? Where's the Messiah? Why isn't my son great, like Elijah, as You said he would be?"

I would imagine if we asked Elizabeth, "What did you think would be best for John to do?" she might say, "Come home, shave, put on some priestly clothes, and put yourself in a position to announce the Messiah." The truth is, mothers don't always know what's best.

What was Jesus' opinion of John? Luke 7:24–28 gives us a glimpse: "What did you go out to see? A man dressed in soft clothing? Those who are splendidly clothed and live in luxury are found in royal palaces! But what did you go out to see? A prophet? Yes, I say to you, and one who is more than a prophet. This is the one about whom it is written, 'Behold, I send My messenger ahead of You, who will prepare Your way before You.' I say to you, among those born of women there is no one greater than John; yet he who is least in the kingdom of God is greater than he."

The nontraditional, atypically dressed preacher was the one about whom Jesus said no one born of a woman was greater. You can't get a better affirmation of a person than that.

God's Higher Ways

It's easy for us to read about another person's child and say, "Of course, God knows best." However, what happens when it's our child who isn't following what we consider the best career path? What if it's our child who is being outspoken about his or her spiritual convictions to the point of offending others? What if it's our child sitting in prison for taking a scriptural stand on moral convictions? How easily do we then relinquish what we think is best in favor of God's will for our child?

We can never, on this side of heaven, fully understand God's ways. Why? Isaiah 55:9 explains: "As the heavens are higher than the earth, so are My ways higher than your ways and My thoughts than your thoughts."

We may think of God's "higher" ways in terms of His being wiser than we are. However, the Hebrew word used in this verse implies more. It means "to be exalted, lofty, of Jehovah's ways—good sense."[1] In other words, even though much of life doesn't make sense to us, our responsibility is to walk by faith, not by sight (2 Corinthians 5:7) and to pray without ceasing (1 Thessalonians 5:17).

My friend Nicki Carlson testifies to God's ways being higher than hers and shares how she learned that God, not mother, truly knows best.

Growing up with a wonderful mother, I always believed in the adage "Mother knows best." After I gave birth to and began raising my two beautiful daughters, I experienced firsthand that there are some things a mother "just knows," and that only a mother knows.

My confidence in my own maternal instinct, however, would never be so shaken as it was when my family and I began traveling down a long and twisted road of foster parenting. God had given us a definite directive to complete our family and begin seeking our son, the one He had set aside for us to adopt. It was a difficult and emotional process of uncertainty, questioning, growth, and faith. And then one day, just hours after an out-of-the-blue phone call, there he was: this tiny baby boy, asleep in a car seat on our living-room floor.

Our son came to us as an emergency foster placement, meaning we took him into our home not knowing if he would be with us for a night, a month, or years. With all our hearts we wanted him forever, from the moment we saw him.

I learned time and again over the course of that next year that this momma does not know best. So many obstacles arose and events transpired while our son was with us before his adoption—circumstances I would never have chosen for him. Serious health problems and developmental delays, biological-family issues, legal issues, government-agency issues . . . it was like being in the middle of a hurricane with debris flying all around us. We would try to grab hold of something and inch our way forward, only to have something new come flying at us. We were so obviously not in control of this massive storm, but luckily we knew who was. This hurricane was filtered through the hands of our son's heavenly Father, who was protecting him and securing a future for him.

My knees were worn out from praying next to that baby's crib. So many times I didn't even know what to pray but just cried out to God to protect and bring to fulfillment every aspect of His perfect plan for this child's life. I prayed Jeremiah 29:11 over him every day, knowing that only God knew this child's future. I didn't even know what I wanted half the time because my understanding and knowledge were so limited. Had I been able to eliminate, for example, the painful health problems he was experiencing, he might not have ended up in our home at all. I loved this child so unconditionally that I prayed that even if God wanted him to be with another family, to make that happen. I only wanted God's perfect will for this precious boy, no matter what kind of toll it took on me.

I know that before my son, I really did believe "Mom knows best." Boy, was I wrong. Some of the very things I hoped for would have resulted in the loss of my son. I was fighting for control over my children with the Creator of the universe and actually had the audacity to think I knew better, that I could protect them from getting hurt. Truth is, I never really had that desired control in the first place, and if I did, I would have totally screwed everything up.

God had a plan for our son that was far better than we could even imagine. Two years later he is a happy, healthy, energetic little boy who has completed our family. All I have to do is look back at the difficulties God has brought us safely through to know that He is working all things together for our good. And that is a wonderful thing to remember as my son's story, and ours, continues to unfold before Him.

When Bad Things Happen

I wouldn't dare tell you that everything that happens to our children is-God ordained. I don't believe it is. God does not ordain physical, sexual, verbal, or emotional abuse of children. God does not ordain child pornography. God does not ordain the child slave trade. God does not wish upon your children sickness or car accidents, rape or murder. Our Plan B world, under the reign of Satan, is filled with the fallout from sin—which is the very reason Jesus came, to redeem us from Satan's tyranny. Unfortunately, sometimes our children will suffer for the cause of righteousness. This is what happened with Elizabeth's son John.

God's higher way was for John to be His mouthpiece, to preach Scripture, call people to repentance, and prepare the way for Christ. In the line of duty, he offended Herod Antipas, who had married his half brother's wife, Herodias. John spoke against their sin, much to Herodias's dislike. At Herod's birthday dinner, Herodias's daughter danced for Herod and his guests. Herod was so pleased that he indulgently promised her whatever she wanted. At her mother's prompting, she asked for the head of John the Baptist on a platter that very night. Though grieved at this request, Herod complied. "He sent and had John beheaded in the prison" (Matthew 14:10).

Matthew 14:11 continues, "And his head was brought on a platter and given to the girl, and she brought it to her mother." We won't go into the wrong, sick, evil parenting practices of Herodias, nor the scarring it must have left on her daughter's soul.

Was Elizabeth still alive? If so, how did she hear the news? Did the disciples who took John's body, buried it, and reported to Jesus what had happened also report to her? We don't know about Elizabeth, but we do know about Jesus. When he heard about John, "He withdrew from there in a boat to a secluded place by Himself" (Matthew 14:13). Although Jesus knew John would live forever in God's presence, He mourned his cousin's death and the evil that caused it.

Not the End of the Story

Often, with our mom-vision, our child's present predicament is all we can see. However, the Bible is filled with story endings that our minds often fail to consider in our own circumstances. God's higher ways bring ultimately good endings. Elizabeth's son doesn't remain headless in the grave. He is alive in God's presence and, for a change, is eating a heavenly feast instead of locusts. He enjoys fellowship with those who responded to his call to repent. He is united with his earthly parents, Elizabeth and Zacharias. He is in the presence of Gabriel, who announced his birth and mission. He is with his cousin Jesus—his High Priest, Savior, and Lord. His eyes see that which we have not seen.

Peter, who stood in Christ's presence during His transfiguration and saw Moses and Elijah with Him, wrote this: "We ourselves heard this utterance made from heaven when we were with Him on the holy mountain. So we have the prophetic word made more sure, to which you do well to pay attention as to a lamp shining in a dark place, until the day dawns and the morning star arises in your hearts" (2 Peter 1:18–19).

Plan A Mom Tip

Adopt the attitude that our heavenly Father, not mom, knows best. Be alert and open to God's higher plans for your children.

Was the burly fisherman simply waxing poetic, or is he telling us something to which we should pay attention?

I'm convinced he's telling us to believe. That he has been on the holy mountain, and he saw those who had been dead, alive. Peter says we do well to pay attention—that a new day will dawn for our children and all who believe.

LIVE OUT LOUD

Plan A Mom Checkup

Ask yourself the following questions to help you disarm the land mine of thinking you know better than God what is best for your children.

1. When things don't go according to your plans, do you prayerfully go to God and acknowledge to Him that you recognize His ways are higher than yours? Do you bow before the Almighty and submit to His ways?
2. Confess to your heavenly Father if you have been adamant that your way is the only way.
3. When your child does something differently than you would have done it, are you convinced it's the biggest mistake in the world and he or she is off track and outside of God's will?
4. Ask God to show you and your children His higher ways.

LOVE OUT LOUD

1. What would have been your response if God had impressed you to name your child something other than what you had planned?
2. What thoughts would have run through your mind when your son headed for the desert instead of the synagogue?
3. What speaks to your heart about Jesus' comments about John?
4. What parenting truth do you want to take from the account of Elizabeth and John?
5. What do you want to "take home" from Nicki's testimony regarding her son?
6. Memorize Isaiah 55:9. Teach it to your children. Share it with your adult children through conversation or an e-mail, text, or card. Post it on Facebook or Twitter as a reminder and encouragement to others. Share it with another mother as a word of encouragement to her.

BETWEEN YOU AND GOD—PRINCIPLE TO REMEMBER

I defuse the land mine of thinking I know what's best for my children by trusting that God's ways are higher than my ways.

Father, thank You that You have a plan for my children's lives. Thank You that Your plans are good and righteous and holy. Help my children to follow Your plans. In Jesus' name, amen.

LAUGH OUT LOUD

I walked into the living room, where Johnathan was playing with his toy cell phone. He had a very serious look on his face and promptly told me, "Mom, you need to call the doctor. The monkeys are jumping on the bed."—Nicki Carlson

11

BLAMING GOD OR KNOWING GOD'S PEACE

I defuse the land mine of blaming God for my child's death
by looking to Him for peace.

I will lift up my eyes to the hills; from whence shall My help come?
My help comes from the Lord, who made heaven and earth.

Psalm 121:1

Without doubt, of all the Plan Bs a mother experiences, most devastating is the death of a child. I cannot imagine such grief.

I have been with my mama, daddy, and mother-in-law when they breathed their last breath on earth and entered heaven. It was so obvious that although their body remained, their soul had departed. It wasn't just that they weren't breathing. It was a genuine before and after: the soul enlivening their bodies, and then the soul being gone. The apostle Paul spoke well when he explained that to be absent from the body was to be at home with the Lord (2 Corinthians 5:8).

Absent from the Body, Home with the Lord

In 2 Corinthians 5:6, 8–9, Paul's choice of the word *absent* is significant. The Greek word he uses for "absent" is *ekdemeo*, which means to go abroad, emigrate; to be or live abroad.[1]

Other times, such as 2 Corinthians 10:1, 11 and 13:2, 10, he uses the Greek word *apeimi*, which means to go away, depart.[2]

This is of huge significance. Paul explains that when our loved ones die, they aren't gone in the sense of being nonexistent. Rather, they've "emigrated"—left this country, moved abroad, and are living there. Where are they living? Children and those of an age of accountability who have repented of their sins and accepted Christ as Savior are living with the Lord. "We are of good courage, I say; and prefer rather to be absent from the body and to be at home with the Lord" (2 Corinthians 5:8).

Have you ever traveled abroad or gone on vacation? As much as you enjoyed it, wasn't it nice when you returned home to your own bed? Throughout the Bible, we're told that this earth is not our real home. The believer's citizenship is in heaven. That's why we're often uncomfortable with our lives; why everything seems discordant. It's why we feel ourselves in unfamiliar territory in this world.

Paul saw what we've not yet seen. He had a vision, a revelation of what he called the "third heaven." He explained that he doesn't know if he was dead and went to heaven or if it was a near-death experience, but he saw a vision of heaven. Whichever it was, he was "caught up into Paradise and heard inexpressible words" (2 Corinthians 12:4).

He goes on to speak of his experience in terms of "the surpassing greatness of the revelations" (2 Corinthians 12:7). Therefore, when Paul writes of preferring to be absent from this earth and body to live abroad with Jesus, he speaks with authority that it is a surpassingly better place to live.

Bereaved Mothers in the Bible

Throughout the Bible we read accounts of mothers whose children died:

- Elizabeth—As we studied in the previous chapter, John the Baptist was cruelly executed, his severed head served on a platter under the tyrannical reign of Herod Antipas.
- Bethlehem mothers—Herod the Great (father of Herod Antipas), in a jealous attempt to kill Christ, the newborn King about whom he had heard, ordered the slaughter of all baby boys two years old and under in the vicinity of Bethlehem.

- Mary—The mother of Jesus certainly would not have considered her son's arrest, scourging, and crucifixion any kind of Plan A. It could not possibly have been in her mind that her son, God's Son, would die at age thirty-three, and in such a torturous, unjust way.

A Grieving Mother's Hope

Since I've never experienced the loss of a child, I asked two friends, whose children have died, to share their testimonies with you. The first account is from Lanie Ebelt. Her only daughter, Stacey, died unexpectedly at age nineteen. The second story is that of my son's mother-in-law, Lindy Neuhaus. One of her children, Bo, died at age twelve after a two-and-a-half-year struggle with cancer. These mothers suffered greatly but want their testimonies to encourage and help you or someone you know who may have a child near death or one who has recently gone to be with the Lord.

I never planned to lose such a precious gift. Cute, cuddly, pink, and the biggest brown eyes you ever saw. She said she would have three children. I dreamed of being a grandmother. That was MY plan. I never considered there could be another plan. Then one day, in 1993, I received a call from the hospital in Boca Raton. There had been an accident. I left work and met my husband at the emergency room.

We learned that our daughter had suffered two strokes: one in class and another after she arrived at the hospital.

A stroke? She was only nineteen.

Doctors told us that along with several issues in her physical makeup, the birth-control pills she was taking to lighten heavy periods were the likely culprit. I have tried many times to explain that she was not sexually active—wasn't even seeing anyone at the time. I had been with her to the doctor. She had been smoking, and I had asked the doctor to tell her not to smoke while on the pills. I was afraid of cancer, not a stroke.

Stacey was in an induced coma for a week. Then, for another week, she was in the hospital but improving daily. Paralyzed on her left side, she was scheduled for therapy. Hospital staff asked us not to be there during the day due to the pressure it put on her to "perform." We went about our day and then, after work, spent each evening at the hospital. On Wednesday Stacey walked for the first time since her stroke. That evening we had a great visit. Her dad told her he was going out of town but that I would be there Thursday. I hugged her good-bye, told her I loved her a whole lot and how proud I was of her accomplishments toward recovery, and left for the night. I didn't know I had said good-bye to my daughter for the last time. While doing her therapy on Thursday, she collapsed to the floor and never recovered. She'd had a blood clot in the upper part of her body, and when she became mobile again, it moved to her heart. They tried to revive her, but she was gone.

Gone, too, were my dreams of a beautiful bride, handsome son-in-law, and three grandchildren. My Plan A had become a tragic Plan B. But God is so good. He has sustained me these seventeen years. He has taught me to live for today and let Him take care of tomorrow. I learned also to give my son to Him each day because I do not know what tomorrow will hold. God showed me how important it is to tell people that you love them.

I've been asked many times what I did after Stacey was gone. I have to say, I was in shock. Also, maybe depression. We were moving back to Detroit, and I had to get the house ready to sell. Plus I had a sixteen-year-old son and needed to make sure he was dealing with the loss of his sister. All I know is I had confidence in God that we were going to get through this with His power.

While Stacey's death was tragic, many good things have come out of that tragedy. A friend of hers who was not a Christian came faithfully to see Stacey in rehab. Many times she would bring her boyfriend, so I got to know him also. After Stacey died, we stayed in touch. They eventually married and had children. One day this young woman called me, knowing how I felt about the importance of raising children in church, and asked me what she should do. I suggested that she and her husband visit churches to find one they liked. One day she called to say she had found a church and that even her husband was enjoying going. The next thing I knew, she called me and said they had accepted Christ as their Savior. I am still in contact with her today.

I know that what I said or did was not the reason they were saved. But I do believe the world observes how we believers live. We make a difference in others' lives every time we come in contact with them. What we say and do has an affect on people. Stacey talked with her friends about God. After her funeral, one young woman came to me because, during the service, the question was asked: "Do you *know where you will spend eternity?" She told me she couldn't answer that question and that Stacey was the only person who had talked to her about Christ. Had she not been Stacey's friend, she wouldn't have been at the funeral to hear those words. She asked me if I would tell her how to be saved. She came to our house, and we led her to the Lord. I still keep up with her.*

In 1991 Stacey took a creative writing class. Their assignment was to write a letter to a soldier in Desert Storm. She became pen pals with a young man named Mike, and they wrote faithfully to one another. He came home on leave and came to meet Stacey. They hit it off, and when he got out of the service, they continued to write. He moved back to the Detroit area intending to pursue a romance with her, and he was heartbroken to learn she was gone. I stayed in contact with him, and one day he said he was thinking about selling his house and going back to school full time. He asked if he could move in with us and commute to college. We talked it over, and soon he became a part of our family. We felt that, although we had lost Stacey, God had given us another son. Some time later, I asked him if he would go to church with us. He did, and he loved it. He had not been raised in church, so it was a new experience for him. He made friends quickly and began going to Bible study. Soon after, he accepted Christ as his Savior and was baptized. It was one of the most wonderful occasions in my life. Shortly after that, he met the girl he would marry—a wonderful Christian. We are still together as "family," and I even get to have their five kids as "grandchildren" in my life.

You could never convince me that our lives are not planned out by a God who loves us. So much of what I lost when Stacey died, He has restored to me through this family. God loves us, and He knows our every need.

Lanie's testimony is a witness that God will give supernatural strength for a grieving mother to keep putting one foot in front of the other. Lindy Neuhaus also discovered this. Unlike Lanie's daughter, Stacey, who died suddenly and unexpectedly, Lindy's son suffered for two and a half years with liver cancer. The following excerpts from the book Bo wrote with Lindy, *It's Okay God, We Can Take It*, is but a sample of God's provision in the worst of Plan B.

When we got the news about Bo's type of cancer and that his prognosis was not very good, we were, needless to say, devastated. We resented every doctor who entered Bo's room because each one seemed to only want to tell us more bad news. I have to say, in retrospect, that those doctors were amazing. They were able to relate to us this impending nightmare and yet did not jerk every bit of hope from us . . . .[3]

It is unfortunate that it so often takes a crisis situation to make us stop and take the time to sense God's presence and his grace. The phrase that one hears from a very young age, "the peace that passeth all understanding," is such a powerful truth, but one can't really understand its meaning unless he has experienced that peace. Here we were facing every parent's nightmare, and yet we felt a peace and a love that we had never known . . . .[4]

The word "death" became a part of our vocabulary. We didn't dwell on it, by any means, but we became comfortable with it and this is something that I hope we never lose. Death is the only guarantee any of us have in this life, and yet it is the one thing that we most avoid talking about. . . . Birth is a passage in this life. Isn't death, then, another passage? So why do we not talk about it? It is just as important as birth, and probably more so.

Plan A Mom Tip

We can defuse the land mine of resentment and blaming God for our child's death by looking to God and resting in His peace that passes all understanding.

I believe one of the greatest gifts we can give our children is to relieve them of the fear of death, to teach them that death is not the worst thing that can ever happen to us, and to prepare them. After all, God is the only one who knows when He will call one of his children home.[5]

Amazing testimonies. Whereas blame, resentment, anger, and disillusionment with God could have lingered, these mothers exude an inner strength, purpose, and hope that is literally out of this world.

LIVE OUT LOUD

I considered not including a checkup section in this chapter, worried that it might seem too harsh for such a tender subject. Then I remembered Lanie and Lindy's words, and I think it's time well spent for us to consider the following.

Plan A Mom Checkup

1. How do I think of death: as the end of life or "living abroad," as Paul explained?
2. Do I avoid discussing the subject of death? Or, like Lindy, am I comfortable talking about it as I am talking about birth?
3. Do I shroud myself in the sorrows of missing my deceased child or wear the covering of God's peace?
4. Have I committed my life to Christ? Do I live with the assurance that I will go to my child one day in heaven?

LOVE OUT LOUD

1. What does it mean to you to know that when you breathe your last breath on earth, your life will not end, but you'll live abroad—in heaven?
2. How have Lanie and Lindy's testimonies helped or encouraged you?
3. Lindy shared how she experienced the peace spoken of in Philippians 4:7, "peace that passeth all understanding" (KJV). The Greek word for "passeth" is *huperechó* and means to "be above, be superior in rank, authority, power; to excel, to be superior, better than, to surpass."[6] If you have experienced God's peace that surpasses understanding, briefly share the occasion as a testimony to others of God's faithfulness.
4. What does Philippians 4:7 say God's peace that surpasses understanding will do?

———— ✦ ————

BETWEEN YOU AND GOD—PRINCIPLE TO REMEMBER

I defuse the land mine of blaming God
for my child's death by looking to Him for peace.

Father, thank You for the gift of Your peace that surpasses all understanding. Thank You that my child isn't ever away from Your presence but is alive with You. Thank You that I'll one day be reunited with my child and be with You. In Jesus' name, amen.

———— ✦ ————

LAUGH OUT LOUD

My sister was carrying my daughter, Kim, down the hall of a hospital. Little Kim was looking back and saying, "See the boid!" (bird—she couldn't yet say her *R*s). Gail turned to see what bird could possibly be in the hospital, and there stood three nuns. Kim thought they were penguins.—Sandra Chapman

12

Strong-Willed Child
Despair or Godly Perspective

I defuse the land mine of despairing over my strong-
willed child by adopting God's perspective on my child.

The Lord is near to all who call upon Him, to all who call upon Him in truth.

Psalm 145:18

If you scanned the table of contents and flipped immediately to this chapter, welcome to the Moms of Strong-Willed Children club. We share a bond that other mothers don't. Only we know what it's like to have a strong-willed child; to wonder how the darling in pink, with her hair in pigtails, has the ability to drive us up the wall. We're convinced it would be easier to fight a fire-breathing dragon than clash with our iron-willed offspring.

You might have a strong-willed child if . . .

- You cuddle your child, read bedtime stories, give last sips of water, say prayers, and tuck him into his crib only to have him climb back out. Repeatedly.
- It's not your child but you who's crying when your husband comes home from work.

- The thought has ever crossed your mind that although you love your child, you're not so sure you like her.
- Your child insists on having the last word, even after being warned not to say another word.
- You threaten to throw away all his toys, and he tells you he doesn't want them anyway.
- She spanks *you*.
- Your child thinks he's in charge, not you. And some days, you think so too.
- You start counting to three, and he finishes counting for you.
- It takes more than an hour in time-out before she'll say "I'm sorry."
- She weighs the consequences before acting . . . and decide it's worth it. Meg, at age three, helped herself to candy while my friend was babysitting her. When my friend asked her what her mommy would do, Meg said, "Time-out" and walked over to put herself in time-out. Then she smiled and said, "But it was good." Another shared that when her daughter was not yet a year old, she would walk up to the TV, spank her own tiny hand and say, "NO, NO!" . . . and then proceed to turn all the knobs.
- When you pray the fruit of the Spirit over your five-year-old, he says, "Mom, please don't pray for me to have self-control!"
- When your child is "done" with shopping, he turns to women you pass in the aisle, points, and says, "You're a bad lady." This was enough of an embarrassment to get me to take Brandon home. By the way, he is almost seventeen now and is a sweet, thoughtful guy. God is good. Moms, hang in there!
- After years of wondering why God gave our precious, precocious daughter such a strong will, He answered my question dramatically. When she was eight, I saw her fight her way back to consciousness after a severe head injury. In the ambulance I felt sure I heard God say, "I created her that way for a reason. Don't question My plans for her." And, of course, He knew a weakling would never do for the plans He had for her life.

Survivor Tips for Mothers of Strong-Willed Children

Moms, you are not alone. You have the Lord's wisdom and also the wisdom of others who have experience raising strong-willed children to help you. Following are some positive actions you can take.

Get smart

I'll never forget the day I realized I needed to wise up with my little one. We were in Lubbock, Texas, visiting my parents, and Lauren's strong will surfaced more than once. When my mother could no longer contain herself, she looked me squarely in the eye and said, "Well, I guess Lauren's a lot smarter than you are." Stunned, I couldn't think of anything to say, but I did ponder her words. Was I really letting Lauren get away with too much? Was I not disciplining her enough or in the right way? I made a mental note to wise up—to stay a step ahead of Lauren; to think through her objections and tactics and be prepared to meet them head-on or, better yet, prevent them through more fine-tuned parenting. It helped.

Adopt God's perspective

Seldom do moms prepare for the arrival of their little one by reading James Dobson's *The Strong-Willed Child*. That thought doesn't cross our minds until we have a strong-willed child. Then it takes weeks, sometimes months for us to admit: "My name is _____, and I'm the mother of a strong-willed child." I remember the day I started to read Dobson's book. I'm sure he didn't say it like this, but I got the strong impression that if I didn't get control of my child, and if Lauren didn't make a decision for Christ by the time she was five, she would likely become an out-of-control teen. Dr. Dobson put the fear of God in me for my child's sake.

It wasn't Dobson, though, who changed my perspective toward Lauren. It was God. One morning, during my quiet time before the rest of the family rose, I sat at the breakfast table and confessed to God that I loved Lauren but didn't particularly like her. I'm not sure what I thought He was going to do about it since she was already delivered, but at last I got it off my chest.

God immediately spoke to my heart. It was one of those moments that's clear as a bell. You know it's God because it's not the way you think. "Debbie, I made Lauren the way she is. If you raise her to know Me, she'll never do anything she doesn't want to do. She won't get pregnant out of wedlock. She won't use drugs. She'll be a strong witness for Me."

In those moments of communion with God, He said a whole lot to my heart and my head. First, He comforted me: Lauren's temperament wasn't a mistake. He divinely created her like that. Then He encouraged me: It was for Lauren's good and even the good of others that she had a strong will. God had a plan to use Lauren for His kingdom. God changed my visual of an out-of-control teenage daughter slamming doors by showing me what He saw: a strong, committed teenager, a witness for Christ. I couldn't wait to tackle the challenge of forming my daughter's mind to know and love God. That change in my perspective changed my parenting. It gave meaning and purpose to Lauren's strong will. God's reassurance increased my love for her.

Teach the value of obedience

After God parented me, one of His strong-willed children, who had been fighting Lauren's personality, I began to purposefully help Lauren see the value of obedience. In the mornings and afternoons, when she was ready to look at books, we'd sit on the couch together and I would read Bible stories to her. "Noah obeyed God and built an ark. God was able to save Noah because he obeyed." "Moses obeyed God and went up the mountain. Moses got to write the Ten Commandments because he obeyed God." "God told Jonah to go to Ninevah and tell the people about God's love. Jonah didn't obey God. He disobeyed. A whale swallowed Jonah." Pause. Let that sink in.

Strong-willed children are smart. Teach them the value of obedience. "God likes it when you obey Mommy" became a line of reinforcement, as did, "When you obey, it makes Mommy happy"—followed by big smiles and hugs.

Take time to closely observe your child

It took me a long time to finally "get" this one, but when I did, it made all the difference in the world. Although we love and want to spend quality time with our kids, parent-child relationships are often plagued by hurriedness. "Get your clothes on. Where are your shoes? Time for breakfast. Where's your jacket? Cupcakes for school this morning? Why didn't you tell me last night?" In the process of giving directives and managing our homes, extended family, church, business, ministry, volunteerism, school, extracurricular, and social lives, we can wake up and realize we're not looking deeply into our children's eyes and seeing their souls. Our backs may be to them, getting juice from the refrigerator, when they tell us, "I don't want to go to school." Our rote reply, "Of course you're going to school. It's a school day," may be sufficient to get nine-year-old Johnny in the car. However, what if Johnny is being bullied? What if he doesn't like school because he can't keep up and needs help, or glasses? Sometimes what we interpret as obstinate may be more than just a strong-willed child acting out. Their behavior may have a root cause to which we need to pay attention.

At this point, some of you may be feeling guilty. "I didn't realize my child was dyslexic. If I had paid more attention . . ." Or, "I didn't realize she was sick. I just thought she was being whiny." I doubt there's a mom out there who doesn't have a regret—or a whole sack full of them. Let's take care of that right now. Take that regret and lay it at the feet of Jesus. If you're like me, you might say something like, "Lord, I just didn't realize. I'm so sorry." Once you've done that with a sincere heart, move on. It's never too late to be a better parent.

Take time not just to be with your children but also to closely observe them. Watch them when they don't know you're watching them. What is their countenance? When they're bullying little brother, what is their expression? Are they angry or sad? What do their eyes tell you? Are they tired? I think far too often we wear out our children with endless activities and schedules when their little bodies and minds need time to relax or have unstructured time. Pay attention to the cues they're sending.

Give choices

The strong-willed child has the potential to be a leader and influence others for Christ. Instead of repressing their leadership tendency, find ways to reinforce their God-given potential. If possible, never back a strong-willed child into a corner. If you do, he or she will just come out fighting. Rather, offer choices. "Would you like to clean your room and then go to the park, or clean your room and then get ice cream?" "Do you want cereal or eggs?" "Do you want to have Johnny or Jim come for a visit after school?" "Do you want to wear the red or blue sweater?" "Do you want to read this book or that book?"

It takes a little more thought and creativity to give two positive options, but it's well worth the effort. In the long run, you'll spend far less energy than you would in a battle of wills.

Allow consequences

At times, two good options don't exist. We can make those teachable moments, when we tell our children the truth, the potential results of their choices, and let them learn consequences. This hurts us and our children if they choose wrong and have to suffer the consequences. But if we can teach them to trust us and that warnings are for their good, we'll build a lifelong relationship of trust and respect. That trust and respect will help carry your strong-willed child (and you) through the tween and teen years, and you'll have a far better relationship than it might otherwise be.

I remember when Lauren was around five years old. She was taking tap dance lessons at Peggy Anne's and was practicing her shuffle hop step. The only problem was, she was practicing it barefoot on the top level of the wooden play gym Keith had built. I was sitting in the backyard watching. "Lauren, don't do a shuffle hop step barefoot on the wood. You'll get a splinter." No choices, just a mom calling out a command. "Put your shoes on." Lauren looked me in the eye, grasped the handrail, and did a big shuffle—then let out a scream. I ran to her, grasped her in my arms, and took her in the house. There, lodged in the ball of her foot, was the largest splinter I'd ever seen. I'm squeamish and wanted nothing to do with dislodging it, but I had no choice. It came out fairly easily, but not without further pain to Lauren. Loving on her, I tenderly explained, "Lauren, that's why I told you not to do a shuffle hop step." Lesson learned. Mommy does know a few more things than daughter . . . a few things that may prevent her from being hurt in the future.

Moms, we have God-given opportunities to gain our children's respect in the little things so that as they grow, we'll have their respect in the bigger things. Lauren learned that day that there's nothing wrong with a shuffle hop step in and of itself. However, it needs to be done in the right place, wearing the right shoes. That lesson, painful as it was for her, laid a foundation for her respecting me when I told her I didn't want her to watch certain television shows because they weren't good for her mind and spirit. She understood that her mom and God wanted to protect her and keep her thoughts pure.

Pray

I cannot overemphasize the importance of prayer. We moms pray that our children's hearts will be tender, that they will be teachable, that they will yearn to know and obey the Lord, that they will respect us. We pray for ourselves to have patience and for wisdom to know how to most effectively discipline our kids. We'll talk more about prayer in a later chapter.

Little lessons. Little consequences. Teachable moments. Building respect. Loving. Watching. All these and more were what Mary, Jesus' mother did with her strong-willed son.

Jesus, a Strong-Willed Child

Perhaps you've never thought of Jesus as being a strong-willed child. I beg to differ.

The only account we have of His tween years is when He decided, apart from His parents, that He would stay in Jerusalem rather than go home with them. No doubt Jesus knew when the family caravan was leaving town. He simply didn't want to go. Later, when Mary confronted Him, He explained that He was in His Father's house (Luke 2:48–49). Jesus wasn't rude to her. He was forthright and honest. His mother wanted Him with her and His earthly father. Jesus wanted to be in His heavenly Father's house. How hard it must have been for Jesus to leave the heights of Jerusalem and go "down with them" (Luke 2:51) to the carpenter's shop in Nazareth.

Jesus' strong will is evident not only in what He did but also in what He didn't do. He's our model of a strong-willed individual standing against fleshly desires and being obedient to His Father's will. When Jesus could have called down legions of angels at His arrest, He didn't. When Jesus could have come down off the cross, He didn't. Why? Because His strong will was subjected to His Father's will. "He said, 'Behold, I have come to do Your will'" (Hebrews 10:9).

Mary's Model for Raising Strong-Willed Children

Mary faced challenges such as we'll never know. When this young mother must have been at wits' end, her son wasn't. "Why do I always get in trouble and Jesus doesn't?" her other children must have complained. "Because He's God. That's why!"

What I learn from Mary is that she was thoughtful. Sure, she probably felt run ragged, like moms do at times. No doubt she fell into bed exhausted at night. She may not have understand why, how, or what regarding a situation, but she didn't let it pass her by without thinking it through. I think, in addition to her purity and willing obedience, that's why God chose her to bear His Son. We see this thoughtfulness in Mary in Luke 2:19, after the shepherds visited them at Jesus' birth: "Mary treasured all these things, pondering them in her heart." We see it again in Luke 2:51, in her response to Jesus' explanation of why He'd stayed behind in the temple in Jerusalem: "His mother treasured all these things in her heart."

The Greek word translated "treasure" in Luke 2:19 is *suntereo* and means to keep within one's self, or keep in mind (a thing, lest it be forgotten).[1] The Greek word used in Luke 2:51 is *diatereo* and means to keep continually or carefully.[2]

I think it's important that we ponder what is happening with our children rather than brush by events and what our children do or say. My friend Dena Dyer shared her experience as a first-time mom of a strong-willed child. Dena, who loves to encourage women through writing, speaking, and singing and is the author of several books, hundreds of articles, and dozens of essays, speaks wise words to moms:

Like many first-time moms, before my oldest son was born, I had a clear idea of my future parenting world. I pictured a happy, intelligent, godly child who would love and obey me—with a sunny attitude. I also imagined that I would be patient, kind, and firm but loving. I planned on never, ever yelling at, spanking, or bribing my child.

Jordan took a grenade to those ideas within the first few days of his arrival. He had trouble nursing, colic, and lots of ear infections. I ended up suffering from severe postpartum depression, and every day seemed to last for months. Though medicine and counseling helped me through the initial frightening weeks of motherhood, my world shattered again when Jordy reached toddlerhood. His strong will—and mine—clashed hourly. Many days my husband came home to find both of us in tears. I remember one particularly black day when I'd tried every trick in my book and gotten nowhere. I'd come very close to slapping Jordy, and it shook me.

At the time I didn't know anyone who had experience the "strong-willed child" phenomenon, and I felt so alone. My husband worked long hours, and I often felt like running out the door screaming. The guilt was overwhelming too. It hurt me (and still does) to admit, but during those preschool years, I loved Jordan yet harbored immense anger and resentment toward him. I felt like he had hijacked my life and that he was in control—not me.

Wasn't motherhood supposed to be my highest calling and joy? Weren't the other women in my church telling me, "Treasure them when they're young, dear, because they'll be grown up and be gone before you know it"? I knew something was dreadfully wrong with me as a mom. After all, sometimes I couldn't wait for Jordan to grow up. It made me sad, weary, and frustrated beyond words.

Finally my sweet, godly mother sent me a CD from Focus on the Family about strong-willed children. I cried and cried as I listened to it. I didn't feel alone anymore—and I knew I wasn't crazy. Jordy was a particular kind of kid, and I realized that if we could harness his will and direct it into something good, he could become a wonderful leader . . . and he might never succumb to peer pressure!

Things didn't change overnight—at least not with Jordan's behavior. But my perspective changed, and I shared my struggles with a prayer group and with other moms, who helped me persevere. My husband and I began to pray daily, "Lord, break his will, not his spirit." We threw the typical parenting advice out the window and we began instead to use natural consequences and creative tactics to capture Jordan's heart and bind it to ours (and the Lord's). I learned his "love language" (quality time) and began to plan times when he and I could do fun things together—go to a theme park, attend a musical, take a road trip. His dad did the same.

Slowly, Jordan grew in obedience. Inch by painful inch, we made progress. And by the time he was nine or ten, I could honestly say that I was having tons of fun with him. Now, at age twelve, Jordan is a happy, intelligent, godly young man with a heart for the underdog (typical of strong-willed children) and many gifts. He still tests us from time to time, and he loves tormenting his younger brother. We're approaching the teenage years with a good bit of fear and trembling.

But my fellow moms, if you're reading this, I just want you to know that there is hope. Having a strong-willed kid isn't the end of the world. There's a light at the end of the tunnel—and it's not a train.[3]

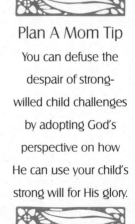

Plan A Mom Tip

You can defuse the despair of strong-willed child challenges by adopting God's perspective on how He can use your child's strong will for His glory.

Following the Golden Rule with Your Strong-Willed Child

God's Word speaks loudly on the subject of how we're to treat our children in what we also know as the Golden Rule: "Treat others the same way you want them to treat you" (Luke 6:31). In other words,

- If you want your children to be loud with you, be loud with them.
- If you want your children to be grumpy toward you, be grumpy with them.
- If you want your children to complain and whine, complain and whine around them.
- If you want your children to rudely interrupt you, rudely interrupt them.
- If you want your children to talk back to their father, talk back to their father.
- If you want your children to grab things, grab things from them.
- If you want your children to scowl and frown, scowl and frown.
- If you want your children to be unhappy, be unhappy.
- If you want your children to be ungrateful, be ungrateful.

However,

- If you want your children to be happy and pleasant, be happy and pleasant.
- If you want your children to laugh and smile, laugh and smile.
- If you want your children to say "please," "thank you," and "excuse me," say "please," "thank you," and "excuse me."
- If you want your children to be kind, be kind.

The list could go on.

As Christian parents, we have an advantage over our children. We have age and years of maturity to know how to pray, listen to God, and problem-solve. We know we have Christ in us and His power and that we can yield our lives to Him. Our infants, toddlers, young children, and even teens either don't yet have those resources or don't have our years of experience of trusting and relying on God. Let's show them Christ in us and model the joy of living by God's Spirit.

LIVE OUT LOUD

Plan A Mom Checkup

1. Am I in a state of despair or prayerfully pondering God's perspective and potential for my strong-willed child?

2. Which do I do more: yell or pray?

3. When my toddler misbehaves, do I get into a battle of wills, or do I correct and then divert his or her attention to something positive?

4. Do I spend more time criticizing my child for wrong behavior or watching for and reinforcing good behavior?

5. Do I model the behavior, tone of voice, countenance, and relational skills I want my child to adopt?

6. Do I have clearly stated guidelines and consequences? Does my child know I will firmly, consistently hold them accountable in love?

LOVE OUT LOUD

1. To which of the "You Might Have a Strong-Willed Child If" scenarios did you most relate?

2. Which of the "Survivor Tips for Mothers of Strong-Willed Children" are helpful to you?

3. What advice from friends of strong-willed children have you found helpful?

4. Read Psalm 145:18. How does this verse encourage you?

5. What other verses encourage you as you parent a strong-willed child?

6. Consider the Bible and how it reinforces who we are in Christ rather than condemning us. What can you learn from that? In other words, how will telling a teen, "Thank you for calling to let me know you would be late," be more effective than belittling him by saying, "You're always late!" Why does praising a toddler for eating her food trump scolding her for not eating it?

7. What "bottom line" verse or thought can you take from this chapter to help you parent your strong-willed child?

BETWEEN YOU AND GOD—PRINCIPLE TO REMEMBER

I defuse the land mine of despair over my strong-
willed child by adopting God's perspective on my child.

Father, thank You for my child and for Your perspective concerning him/her. Thank You that You have a purpose for my child. Give me wisdom and insight to parent my children so they'll grow to love, obey, and serve You. Help me to be mindful that the way I treat them will be the model for how they treat others. In Jesus' name, amen.

LAUGH OUT LOUD

When Kayla was six, she always carried a Hello Kitty notepad with matching pens. One day my husband took her to the store with him and became engrossed in a conversation with a fellow pharmacist. Kayla, who found a large rubber ball she wanted, kept tugging on her dad's arm, but he wasn't paying attention to her. So she wrote him a note—"Buy me the ball or I run away"—and slipped it in his hand. He read it and immediately bought her the ball! (I wouldn't have, but he did.) Kayla is twenty-five now, and her daddy still carries that little note in his wallet.—Phyllis Cook

13

STUBBORNLY INFLEXIBLE OR SACREDLY FLEXIBLE

I defuse the land mine of stubborn inflexibility by
being sacredly flexible in God's hands.

Behold, the bondslave of the Lord; may it be done to me according to your word.

Luke 1:38

The Bible is, in addition to other things, a record of God's dealings with mothers; of His intervening in their lives. He answered their pleas to have children, though not always in their timing. He gave strength to the fainthearted who raised their children without the help of the child's father. He comforted those who grieved the death of their children. He called mothers to acts of faith in their everyday lives.

The mothers in the Bible who stand out as examples are those who lived in communion with God. They didn't operate solo outside of God's will. They were sensitive to His leading. For instance, consider God's involvement with the following mothers:

- Sarah, to enable her to have a child in her old age;
- A widow in Zarephath, miraculously providing for her so that she could provide food for the prophet Elijah and her son;
- Elizabeth, to bless her with a child who would usher in the Messiah.
- Mary, who miraculously bore our Lord Jesus . . . and then had to flee to Egypt to escape Herod's murderous plot.

The list continues, but I want us to focus on one mother in particular, our Lord's.

Flexible or Inflexible

What we notice about Mary is her sacred flexibility. She consents to become pregnant by the most unconventional means. Could she have crossed her arms and said, "No way"? What if she had said to the heavenly messenger, "I'm engaged to Joseph and simply can't get pregnant now"? But Mary didn't say those things. Instead, she said, "Behold, the bondslave of the Lord; may it be done to me according to your word" (Luke 1:38).

Her opportunity to practice being flexible didn't stop with that confession and act of submission. Near her due date, when she probably would have preferred to stay near home, she and Joseph had to go to Bethlehem on a government-mandated business trip. Flexible or inflexible? She went.

There we find Mary and Joseph combing the streets for a hotel. Keep flexing, Mary. How about a stall? I suppose Mary could have crossed her arms and said, "I'm NOT having a baby in a stall, with manure all around!" Yet it was the only shelter available.

After the hard journey to Bethlehem, the strain of searching for a place to stay, and going through labor giving birth to Jesus, Mary must have been beyond exhaustion. How did she respond when Joseph said, "Mary, there are shepherds who want to come in and see Jesus"?

"Dirty shepherds in from the fields? Joseph, no!" Is that what Mary said? No. Perhaps no woman better prophesied over herself than when she had said to the angel, "Behold, the bondslave of the Lord."

Are we yet able to grasp how God was able to daily, moment-by-moment, use this mother because she was flexible? She was not spineless or weak. It took the strongest of women to bear the harsh criticism of an out-of-wedlock pregnancy, withstand the journey to Bethlehem, deliver her baby in a stable, raise the Son of God and then let Him go . . . all the way to the cross.

Being sacredly flexible is not synonymous with weakness. It's experiencing the greatness of God by yielding your body, mind, and soul as instruments to Him. You and I may think of daily activities as ho-hum. But the daily becomes divine when it's marked with God's presence and Spirit. In order for our days to be touched with the glory of God, we must be in communion with Him and sensitive to the Spirit's leading. This begins with opening our eyes to His presence in the mornings. It continues as we offer our bodies to His service and respond to His promptings throughout the day. We stay sacredly flexible in God's hands when we face a difficulty with a child and turn to Him in prayer, listening for His guidance on how to handle our situation.

Sacred Flexibility

We see why God chose Mary. And we can learn from her sacred flexibility.

As a betrothed couple, and prior to Mary's becoming pregnant with Jesus, Joseph and Mary had perhaps talked about what they would name their children. However, Luke 2:21 tells us they didn't get to select the name. God chose it. "His name was then called Jesus, the name given by the angel before He was conceived in the womb." Sacredly flexible or stubbornly inflexible?

It's the middle of the night. You're sound asleep. Suddenly you're shaken awake by your husband, who whispers urgently: "Get up. Get Jesus. We have to leave now!"

"Why? What's going on, Joseph? We can't just leave without telling anyone where we're going." Mary could have been inflexible. Instead, she left with Joseph and Jesus for Egypt in the dark of night even as Herod plotted to have his soldiers kill all the male boys, two years old and under, in the vicinity of Bethlehem.

I'm sure Mary never expected to live in Egypt or raise her family there. No doubt she missed her family. However, instead of doing what *she* wanted, she obeyed God's voice. She served God's purposes in giving birth to the Messiah and protecting Him through His childhood.

When Herod died, an angel appeared in a dream to Joseph, still in Egypt, and said, "Get up, take the Child and His mother, and go into the land of Israel; for those who sought the Child's life are dead" (Matthew 2:19–20).

"Mary, pack your bags."

"Why, Joseph? Where are we going?" Mary asked.

"Back to Israel."

Sacred flexibility.

We could go on and on showing how God used Mary. Praise God, her heart wasn't hardened to spiritual things. She wasn't so set in her ways that she couldn't sense His direction and respond. She wasn't adamant that she live where she wanted to live. She didn't waste moments or miss opportunities God divinely orchestrated. If Mary had not been flexible, perhaps she would never have encountered the shepherds who validated the angel's announcement, or the wise men who worshipped Jesus and provided the young couple with financial gifts that may well have financed their flight to Egypt. Mary's flexibility was key in sparing Jesus' life from Herod's sword.

I wish I had time to trace for you all the Bible mothers who practiced sacred flexibility. Their lives appear common in many ways. The widow of Zarephath, for example; when we look at her we see a tired, thin, worried mother barely making it. There are no angelic pronouncements here. Just her and her son. She's you. She's me. Slowly she stoops to gather a few small sticks to build a little fire to cook one last meal for her and her son before they die.

A stranger approaches and asks, "Please get me a little water in a jar, that I may drink" (1 Kings 17:10).

"As she was going to get it, he called to her and said, 'Please bring me a piece of bread in your hand. But she said, 'As the Lord your God lives, I have no bread, only a handful of flour in the bowl and a little oil in the jar; and behold, I am gathering a few sticks that I may go in and prepare for me and my son, that we may eat it and die.' Then Elijah said to her, 'Do not fear; go, do as you have said, but make me a little bread cake from it first and bring it out to me, and afterward you may make one for yourself and for your son. For thus says the Lord God of Israel, 'The bowl of flour shall not be exhausted, nor shall the jar of oil be empty, until the day that the Lord sends rain on the face of the earth'" (1 Kings 17:11–14).

Stop here for a moment. You're a mama with one son, and you have zero food in the cabinet or refrigerator. A stranger asks you for water. You don't really want to be bothered, but you can handle giving him a drink. Now, though, he pushes. You tell him you only have enough food for you and your child to eat a meager meal before you die; yet he asks you to serve him first.

Flexible or inflexible?

It turns out she was flexible, which is why, no doubt, God sent Elijah to her home. "She went in and did according to the word of Elijah, and she and he and her household ate for many days. The bowl of flour was not exhausted nor did the jar of oil become empty" (1 Kings 17:15–16).

I wonder how many divine assignments we miss each week. I wonder, if we were more flexible, if our children would experience more of God's blessings. I wonder if our flexibility and resulting blessings might encourage our children to be more flexible adults.

Mary and the widow of Zarephath experienced spectacular miracles—the kind that make you rejoice and praise God. True, it's hard to be flexible when everything in you wants to just stick to the status quo. However, it's the mothers who are flexible who experience the joy of God in the midst of their day.

My long time friend Pam Couch tells of a time when her Plan A turned Plan B in relation to her son and the city where he moved. Are relocations something in which God is interested? If you answered no, you haven't been paying attention. Relocations are often, in the Bible, where we see God most involved in people's lives. He's in the business of divine orchestration. Placement of His saints is important for their protection, blessing, fulfillment of His will, and doing the good works He's prepared for us to do (see Ephesians 2:9–10). Here's Pam's story:

> Have you ever started your day with a specific plan and ended up in a completely different place? I think all of us can relate. At times it seems the only thing on which we can depend is that our Plan A will ultimately fall somewhere between B and Z. Two changes in my plans illustrate this.
>
> Plan A for our son, Daniel, was working out just as we had hoped. He graduated from college in four years and was offered his dream job with a large bank in New York City. In addition, he was given the opportunity to serve with Mission Emanuel for seven months in the Dominican Republic before starting his job training. That was the icing on the cake. Plans were set for his ultimate move to New York. He found a roommate, sold his car, and purchased winter clothing. We were a bit worried about his being be so far away, but we also felt blessed and relieved that our son was embarking on a new adventure that seemed custom-designed just for him.
>
> Four months into his mission work he called to let us know he had received some bad news from the bank regarding his job. He would be moving to Houston rather than New York after his training. Daniel was disappointed; but for us, the thought of his working closer to our home in Dallas was comforting. After talking

together about the change, we all agreed it was a blessing to have any job in our current economy, and we began to focus on the positive aspects of Plan B.

The time for him to return to Texas from the Dominican Republic finally came. He spent a couple of days at home in Dallas, and then we went to Houston to help him locate a place to live. We found the perfect apartment with no problem. It was close to his workplace, and the price was right. He was able to connect with friends, buy a car, and locate potential churches to attend. We returned to Dallas thinking everything had worked out beautifully. When we took him to the airport to catch his plane to New York for training, we thought Plan B was going smoothly. He would be back to Dallas in a month, and we would help him make the move to Houston, where he would start his new career.

In the meantime, since Daniel would be in New York for training, he gave me the okay to help him furnish his new apartment, and I went into high gear. I was in my element collecting things to help prepare his first "nest." The result was that our garage in Dallas was filled with things for his apartment, packed and organized by room and ready to load into the U-Haul. Every detail, from furniture to bathroom accessories, had been taken care of. This had been accomplished in record time, and I found I had a couple of weeks to spare before the scheduled move.

With time on my hands, I began thinking and planning how wonderful it would be to make monthly business trips to Houston and visit Daniel while there. I planned to coordinate these trips with my sister in Victoria to see her more often too, as Houston would be a great meeting place for us. Of course I had planned how wonderful holidays would be with our entire family close together. It would be just a short drive to Houston both for my sister and for our daughter, who was in College Station. Plan B seemed like a dream come true. I couldn't wait.

The next phone call from Daniel was to let us know that things had changed again: due to turmoil in the banking industry, instead of moving to Houston, he would now be staying in New York. He was thrilled and felt he could handle getting settled there if we could just send the rest of his clothes.

I felt as if a storm cloud had burst and was raining on my parade! I went from feeling completely connected to his world to being an outsider. I began to wonder and worry: where would he live, would he be able to find a good church, would *he meet a girl from New York and never come back to Texas? What kind of family holidays could we possibly work out with him so far away?*

Plan A and then Plan B had evaporated with a phone call. Instead of feeling the satisfaction of my plan playing itself out perfectly in Houston, I found myself trying to figure out how to start undoing everything I had so proudly accomplished in the last month. It's not nearly as exciting to try to sell used furniture and stand in line to return items at discount stores as it is to find the wonderful bargains and rejoice in how well things are coming together!

My perfect plan had been changed, and I was left with a decision about how to adjust to the new reality. Isn't that what we find ourselves doing constantly as we live life?

Our change of plans for Daniel was simply a change between two good things, with a good bit of inconvenience in between. Several years earlier, we had faced a change in plans with our daughter, Laura, when she was twelve years old, that was much more challenging.

Laura had always been the picture of health. She excelled at competitive sports—soccer, basketball, and softball. Most of our weekends were spent at sporting events, and her favorite motto was "Forget the doll, give me a ball." Plan A for Laura's interests and talents was centered on sports!

Sometime after her twelfth birthday, we noticed that she was losing her stamina. She developed mysterious rashes and began to have joint problems. Her ankles or knees were swollen constantly but not related to a specific injury. After monthly doctor visits and many tests over the course of a year, she was diagnosed with Crohn's disease. The treatment involved taking steroids and a number of other medications with side effects that were undesirable.

Plan B for treatment of her disease didn't work. Plan C involved surgically removing part of her colon, with no guarantee that the disease would not reappear in another part of the colon almost immediately. We are still in Plan C—thank God, Laura came through the surgery beautifully and is still in remission at age twenty-four. After graduation from Texas A&M, she entered the Physician Assistant program at Texas Tech this year. Her illness had a very real impact on her and what she plans to do with her life. Her changes in plan, from A to C will result in her helping others through her experience with chronic illness.

As I was going from Plan A to Plan C (New York) with my son and Plan A to Plan C (Crohn's disease) with my daughter, God equipped me to handle the unexpected changes with a grace and peace that would not have been possible without Christ. I focused on God's sovereignty by claiming verses such as Psalm 103:15–19, which says, "As for man, his days are like grass; as a flower of the field, so he flourishes. When the wind has passed over it, it is no more, and its place acknowledges it no longer. But the lovingkindness of the Lord is from everlasting to everlasting on those who fear Him, and His righteousness to children's children, to those who keep His covenant and remember His precepts to do them. The Lord has established His throne in the heavens, and His sovereignty rules over all." I claimed verses I had memorized, such as Romans 8:28. I prayed to desire the plans God had for me and my children and found rest in Him.

God doesn't promise that we won't have anxious moments when plans change. However, He offers the gift of His presence and the Helper, the Holy Spirit. Whether plans are changed due to another person's actions, sin, or an unstoppable force of nature, we can look to God. We can take our thoughts captive and submit them to Him.

Plan A Mom Tip

Model sacred flexibility to your children so they will grow up to be sacredly flexible in God's hands.

We have not been left alone. Prayer is a two-way street. We go to God, and He comes to us through the Scriptures and by impressing and confirming His will in our hearts. God doesn't ask us to be other people's puppets. He asks us to be His friends and to serve Him. We can choose to practice sacred flexibility and experience His divine presence leading us in the midst of our days. Or we can stubbornly cross our arms and refuse. Which kind of mother have you been? Which kind of mother do you want to be?

LIVE OUT LOUD

Plan A Mom Checkup

1.   On a scale of 1 to 10, how flexible are you?

2. How might being more flexible and open to God's plans affect you and your children in a positive way?
3. If your child grows up to be like you, will he or she be sacredly flexible?
4. Pray now, and ask God to help you be more open to His plans and flexible in the everyday moments of your life.

LOVE OUT LOUD

1. What does the term *sacred flexibility* mean to you?
2. What did you learn from the examples of Mary and the widow of Zarephath about sacred flexibility?
3. What are some practical ways you could initiate a more "sacredly flexible" attitude and lifestyle?
4. What positive effect do you think it would have on your children if you were more flexible and less rigid?
5. Read John 8:28–29. How did Jesus model sacred flexibility?
6. Read Acts 16:6–10. How did Paul model sacred flexibility?
7. How did Philip model sacred flexibility in Acts 8:26–40?
8. Which verse from today's scriptures do you want to memorize? Why?

BETWEEN YOU AND GOD—PRINCIPLE TO REMEMBER

I defuse the land mine of being stubbornly
inflexible by practicing sacred flexibility in God's hands.

Father, thank You for the many examples of mothers in the Bible and mothers today who are flexible in Your hands. Help me to practice sacred flexibility so my children can see Your glory and grow into sacredly flexible adults. In Jesus' name, amen.

Laugh Out Loud

When we moved to Kerrville, my son was in fourth grade and very upset we were moving. He couldn't understand our desire to get him into a better city and better educational opportunities. After a long Christmas break, he finally attended his new school. I was nervous for him and anxious about how he'd do. After school, he ran home. With pure joy he said, "Momma, you were right. God did want us to move here. Tonight they're having basketball tryouts, and I get to be in them!" He was on cloud nine because, in the city from which we'd moved, I couldn't take him to sports activities due to my work schedule and the driving time. It was wonderful to know that even then he could see God's hand in our move and how God takes care of our needs and desires.—Joanna Brown

14

HOPELESS OR HOPEFUL

I defuse the land mine of hopelessness by placing my
hope in God and His love for my child.

And now, Lord; for what do I wait? My hope is in You.

Psalm 39:7

While you're working hard to influence your children to know and honor
Christ, God is working on you, His child.

You're not able to pour into your child selflessness if you're still selfish. You
can't teach your child to use a kind tone of voice if you bark at others or talk down
to them. You can't teach letting the other person have his choice of toy if you insist
on choosing the restaurant. If you get cranky when you don't get your way, how can
you teach your child to not get cranky when she doesn't get her way? If you overload
your schedule and are too tired to go to church on Sunday morning, how can you
teach your children the value of corporate worship and Bible study?

If you stay up late watching television or sitting at your computer, how can you
teach your children the value of reading and going to bed at an appropriate hour? If
you still can't rise fifteen minutes earlier in the morning to start your day in prayer
and Bible reading, how do you expect your child to value that discipline and learn to
listen for God's voice? If you do everything everyone asks you to do rather than live
by the commitments to which God calls you, how can you teach your children to walk
in the good works God has prepared for them rather than just being indiscriminately

busy? If you're materialistic, your closets and cabinets over stuffed, and you can't refrain from making unnecessary purchases, how can you teach your children financial self-control and the value of saving and giving to others? If you don't take care of your body, how can you teach your children that their bodies are entrustments from God and that we are not our own?

So God works on us. First Thessalonians 5:23 reinforces the truth that God is busy sanctifying us while we attempt to parent our children in sanctifying ways, to help them grow as Jesus grew: in stature and in favor with God and people.

In the process of sanctification, we experience setbacks. God goes through them with us, and we go through them with our children. In those times, it may seem hopeless. But with God on our side, things are never hopeless, because He is the God of all hope.

Jochebed: Hopeless or Hopeful

One mom who may have felt hopeless at times was Jochebed. We discussed her in an earlier chapter, in relation to baby Moses. However, her hopeful/hopeless roller coaster was not confined to events surrounding her most famous son. Her other children, Miriam and Aaron, also took her on a few ups and downs.

Moses

Jochebed's hope in God was well placed when it came to her son Moses. This one-time murderer and fugitive responded to God's call and committed his life to following Him. Literally. From the burning bush to the Shekinah glory, Moses followed God. It didn't mean his life was easy. It did mean he went in the right direction. His anger, which got him in trouble when he killed the Egyptian taskmaster, continued to be a struggle for Moses. God's sanctifying work redeemed him and shaped him into one of the greatest leaders the world has known; yet even then an outburst of anger (hitting the rock instead of speaking to it) prevented him from entering Canaan. Hopeless, hopeful. Moses didn't enter the earthly Promised Land, but God took him to a better place, the eternal promised land of heaven.

Miriam

Big sister Miriam played a significant role in baby Moses' salvation from the Nile. Jochebed knew she could trust her strong-willed daughter to boldly approach

Pharaoh's daughter and offer her as a nursemaid. However, Miriam had a mouth that could both sing God's praises and get her into trouble.

Surely Jochebed's hope would have plunged to see her daughter struck with leprosy. Did she catch it from someone? No, it was a consequence of her mouth, which she just couldn't keep shut. Of course, the deeper issue with which God was concerned was her haughty heart and critical spirit toward Moses. And God called her out on it.

Had Jochebed not warned her daughter that her mouth could get her into trouble one day? I imagine she had. However, this was an area in which Miriam needed to be sanctified. God exposed the leprosy in her heart by manifesting it in her flesh. Rather than Miriam being the "big deal" she thought she was with God and the people, she was the cause of the nation not moving forward for seven days (Numbers 12).

Aaron

Jochebed's younger son, Aaron, grew up as a slave while Moses grew up in the palace. Although Aaron knew his Hebrew heritage, I think she worried about him: he could be easily swayed.

Were Jochebed alive during the Exodus, she would have felt her hope barometer for Aaron drop precipitously. Just when one child was literally on the mountaintop with God, the other hit bottom. Influenced by the pagan culture in which he was raised, Aaron succumbed to the pressure of those around him and made a golden calf for the people to worship. When Moses called him to account for his behavior, Aaron, lying perhaps even to himself, responded: "They said to me, 'Make a god for us who will go before us. . . .' I said to them, 'Whoever has any gold, let them tear it off.' So they gave it to me, and I threw it into the fire, and out came this calf" (Exodus 32:23–24).

Out came a calf? Exodus 32:4 explicitly states that Aaron fashioned a calf with an engraving tool. I can see how this might easily have sent Jochebed into a state of hopelessness for his soul. Yet, Aaron became high priest.

Today's Mom: Hopeless or Hopeful

Have you ever felt hopeless in relation to your children? Following, my sister and spiritual mentor, Linda McConnico, shares her story of hopeless moments and how

God gave her hope. I hope her life's testimony will encourage you, as it does me, to look to the God of all hope.

It's been almost fifty years since the birth of my youngest child—a beautiful, healthy baby boy. His father wanted to name him after his favorite Uncle Buck, so this precious little one began his journey through life as "Baby Buck." From early childhood he had a kind and gentle heart. The youngest of three, he was often the tagalong, trying his best to keep up with his older brother and sister.

I would have fought a mountain lion for the safety of this child. But it wasn't a mountain lion that came after Buck. It was the world. A world full of disappointments and heartaches. A world of sin and temptation. A world I couldn't protect him from.

The early years of his life were spent in a home filled with late-night arguments. Slammed doors. Tears. And finally, divorce. After that, four years of just the kids and me. Lots and lots of challenges. But during those growing-up years, Buck was always a good child.

Then he went off to college on a baseball scholarship, full of excitement for his future. He made excellent grades and was an all-star third baseman. It seemed he was going to escape the tough stuff his older brother and sister were going through. His brother had dropped out of college and joined the Navy, and his sister was struggling with her life. She was (and is) profoundly deaf and had suffered not only from that impairment but also from several surgeries and drug abuse.

Not a day went by that I didn't feel guilty for what they were going through. They were suffering from the bad choices I had made in my life. My hope was that Buck would be okay in spite of me. That was my prayer.

But it wasn't long before I received what would be the first of many late-night, gut-wrenching phone calls. "Mom, baseball is over for me, but don't worry, I'm okay." A shoulder injury. His baseball career . . . his dream . . . ended. As sad as I was for him, I desperately wanted to believe he would be okay. He was a good young man. He loved the Lord! That was my confidence. But loving God doesn't stop the world or Satan from coming at us and our children.

Beer eased Buck's disappointment and sadness for a while. Then, when alcohol wasn't enough, he slipped into the world of drugs. His guilt and shame were magnified because he knew Christ as his Savior.

One night, when the pain became unbearable for him, he called me for what could have been the last time I would hear his voice. "Mom, I can't live like this any longer. I have a gun. I pray I will go to heaven when I kill myself. I couldn't do it without calling you first. I want you to know it's not your fault. I love you with all my heart. I know you'll be all right because of the way you know the Lord."

My mind raced, but the only words that would come out were, "Honey, please wait until morning. Give me a little time to get ready." We hung up. I fell to my knees and cried out to God all night to save my son. He did. Buck made up his mind to try life again. But by now alcohol and drugs owned him.

Now there was no doubt: I had failed my children. How many times the words "if only" came to my mind. I loved Jesus. He was my Savior. How was it possible that I had messed up not only my life but also the lives of my children? I could accept my own unhappiness because I deserved it. But how could I live with the guilt and shame of causing my children such heartache? I remember dreading nighttime because that was usually when Buck's phone calls would come. Wrecks, crying, remorse, jail. Such pain in his voice . . . and I couldn't fix it.

I lived with a smile on my face by day and a dagger in my heart by night. I later realized that the spiritual warfare being waged over my children was also being fought over me. I wish I could tell you that I suddenly realized how much God loved me and my kids and that we all lived happily ever after. But that's not my story. What I did come to realize is that life is hard. That there's much more to this life than just living happily ever after. Through much study and prayer, I began to understand that "my" kids were really God's kids. That He loved them more than I could ever love them. I couldn't (and still can't) fathom a love that big, but I know in the depths of my being that His heart was broken for them just as mine was. Occasionally I would notice that I wasn't sad. I began to embrace a low level of hope.

God began to lovingly take me through His Word, always ending up at the cross. He showed me His Son, Jesus. His child. How God the Father suffered as His child hung on a cross so that my children and I could spend eternity with Him. As the thought that Jesus had been judged for my sin and went to His death on that horrible cross for everything I had ever done wrong began to go deeper and deeper into the core of my being, something began to happen in my spirit. What I had known in my head began to seep into my heart. That low level of hope began to *grow. Hope that my kids would be okay. Hope that even though life would always be hard, there would also be times of joy and peace for them. That God wanted them to have a good life even more than I did. The guilt that I had borne for so long began to decrease as my hope grew stronger and stronger. God poured His love and grace into this mother who had lived so many years with hopelessness in her heart.*

Today I live full of thanksgiving and praise for what God has and continues to do in our lives. My daughter is drug free. My older son has retired from a successful career in the Navy and has a wonderful wife and two grown children. And Buck is married to a great young woman who serves in ministry with him. God has taken his life experiences and used them to minister to countless others.

My story began half a century ago. I have faced many trials since that journey to the cross so many years ago, but I have also found much joy.

"The peace of God which transcends all understanding," guards my heart and mind in Christ Jesus (Philippians 4:7 NIV).

"May the God of hope fill you with all joy and peace as you trust in him, so that you may overflow with hope by the power of the Holy Spirit" (Romans 15:13 NIV).

Lessons in Hope from a Plan A Mom in a Plan B World

Christian moms have reason to hope for their children. Their hope is not based on their parenting skills or on their child's potential but rather on God, who alerts them to the dangers in the world and to His ability to provide for their child.

Open your eyes to the war over your children

Linda said, "I would have fought a mountain lion for the safety of this child. But it wasn't a mountain lion that came after Buck. It was the world. A world full of disappointments and heartaches. A world of sin and temptation. A world I couldn't protect him from."

Only a mother who is ignorant of the Scriptures fails to acknowledge that there's an ongoing battle for her child. However, we must do more than acknowledge the forces of darkness about which the apostle Paul speaks (Ephesians 6:12). We must do more than gloss over Peter's words that the devil prowls like a roaring lion seeking someone to devour (1 Peter 5:8). We must do more than nod our heads when James warns that friendship with the world is spiritual adultery (James 4:4). We must take God's Word seriously and raise our children according to its teachings. Therein is our hope.

Place your hope in God: pray for your children

I don't know a mom who couldn't echo the sentiment, "I hope my children will be okay in spite of me." I've thought that many times. However, we must do more than just hope they'll be okay. Take the next step, as Linda did, and pray. How do we pray when we don't know for sure what to ask, or we don't see a way out? We pray on the basis of who God is. Following is a sample of His attributes taken from 365 A–Z Names, Titles, and Attributes of God.[1]

God's Attribute: Calls into Being That Which Doesn't Exist (Romans 4:17)
Your hopelessness may stem from your child having no interest in church, God, or anything spiritual. Pray, "Lord, You are the God who calls into being that which doesn't exist. Please call into being a hunger in my son for You."

God's Attribute: Captain of the Host (Joshua 5:14–15)
You may feel like Joshua when he was outside the seemingly impenetrable walls of Jericho—that there's no way to penetrate Satan's stronghold on your child. Pray, "Captain of the host of angels, fight for my child, who is bound in sin. Free him from Satan's stronghold."

God's Attribute: Caring Lord (1 Peter 5:7)
You may feel alone; that no one cares about your child besides you. Pray, "Caring Lord, thank You for being concerned for my child. Lavish her with Your care today so she knows unmistakably that You're present with her."

God's Attribute: Counselor (Isaiah 9:6)
Your child may have shut herself off from you. Pray, "Lord, You are the Mighty Counselor. Counsel my teen. Speak to her mind. Reason with her. Help her respond to Your wise counsel."

As you continue to place your hope in God, the Champion, Chief Shepherd, Comforter, Contender for His people, and more, your hope will increase. Do more than just express, "I hope." Pray according to the powerful names of God on behalf of your children.

Be there for your children; hope for them when their hope wanes

Do your children know you're there for them? My mother told me when I went to college that I could call her anytime, no matter the hour. One time I found myself being pressured to do something I didn't want to do: to take a spur-of-the-moment trip with friends to one of their parents' home out of town. I was a freshman, didn't know one of the couples, didn't know their parents, and didn't feel good about it. Finally I told them I had to check with my parents anytime I went out of town. I'm not sure they told me that, but it sounded reasonable. I called Mama at 2 a.m. and in the presence of everyone said, "The group I'm hanging out with wants to go to Amarillo tonight. Is that all right?" Stupid question, and I received just the answer I wanted and needed. Mama knew exactly what I was doing. She may have even said, "Do you want to go?" However, my response to whatever she said was, "Okay. I won't go. I understand." I hung up and said, "I can't go. Take me back to my dorm." You've gotta love a mom you can call at any hour and know she'll be there for you—and not only be there but pray for you. It's a priceless relationship.

Buck knew he could call his mom the night he was contemplating suicide. He even affirmed her walk with God. Do your kids know you have a great relationship with God and that they can talk to you about anything? Do they know you won't fall apart or scream at them but will listen as they give voice to their thoughts?

Discover hope at the Cross

Linda felt hopeless in her Plan B world in relation to her children, but she discovered hope at the Cross. God showed her how much He loved her and her children. Today Linda is a living testimony of the verse she closed her testimony with: "May the God of hope fill you with all joy and peace as you trust in Him, so that you may overflow with hope by the power of the Holy Spirit" (Romans 15:13 NIV).

Linda is blessed to see her children walking with God. Jochebed, on the other hand, probably didn't live to see Moses return to Egypt and marvel at how God used him. Nor did she know what became of Miriam or Aaron. She knew her children's carnal nature and did everything she could to protect them. However, eventually she knew they would make their own decisions for or against God. They would make good choices, and they would make bad choices. They would experience God's mercy. They would also experience the consequences of their sin.

Moses didn't get to go into the Promised Land. Aaron watched three thousand men die as a result of his fashioning the golden calf. Miriam was "shut up" outside the camp for seven days with leprosy because she didn't shut up her mouth (Numbers 12:14).

Where, then, is my hope? My hope is in God. My hope is in God, who is merciful and not finished with us or our children. My hope is in God, who is doing a great work of sanctification in each of us, preparing us for our eternal home.

Moses became one of the greatest leaders of God's people. Aaron became a high priest, leading people to worship the one true God. Miriam used her mouth as a prophetess to speak forth God's truths and to lead the women of Israel with timbrels and dancing, singing praises to the Lord.

Are you hopeless regarding one or more of your children? If so, be encouraged by God's redeeming work in Jochebed's children, Linda's children, and those of countless other mothers.

Look to the Cross for your hope. Meditate on how much God loves your children—to the point of allowing His own Son to die for them. Replace your hopelessness in your child with your hope in God. "And now, Lord; for what do I wait? My hope is in You" (Psalm 39:7).

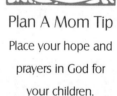

Plan A Mom Tip

Place your hope and prayers in God for your children.

LIVE OUT LOUD

Plan A Mom Checkup

1. On a hopeful/hopeless barometer, how hopeful are you?
2. What have you read that can help you increase your hope?
3. Which attributes of God can you use in prayer as a springboard for your hope?

LOVE OUT LOUD

1. How did God speak to you through our study of Jochebed and her children?
2. Which of the points from "Lessons in Hope from a Plan A Mom in a Plan B World" was helpful? Why? How will you apply it?
3. How does redirecting your mind from the hopelessness of a situation to God's attributes give you more hope?
4. Memorize a verse on hope. Why did you select it? Share the memorized verse with a friend.

BETWEEN YOU AND GOD—PRINCIPLE TO REMEMBER

I defuse the land mine of hopelessness by
placing my hope in God and His love for my child.

Father, thank You for loving my children and me so much that You sent Your Son to the cross on our behalf. Help me to live in the hope of Your great love and power. In Jesus' name, amen.

LAUGH OUT LOUD

When Donnie was in elementary school, he and his brothers constantly played tricks on each other. One afternoon, when Buck was in the bathroom, Donnie found the key, stealthily unlocked the door, flung it open, and jumped toward him with a loud, "BOO!" Only it wasn't his brother in the bathroom: it was his grandmother sitting on the "throne." Was he in for a shock!—Linda McConnico

15

FOCUSING ON MY WEAKNESS OR LIVING BY CHRIST'S EMPOWERMENT

I defuse the land mine of focusing on my weakness
by asking Jesus to help me.

I can do all things through Him who strengthens me.

Philippians 4:13

We often talk about a Plan A mom in a Plan B world in the context of what our child experiences. However, sometimes a Plan A mom's Plan B is related to her own struggle or illness. Such is the case with Melinda Yeary, who has suffered from Multiple Sclerosis for thirty-one years. When I first met Melinda, she was the high-energy wife of Dan Yeary, university minister at First Baptist Church in Lubbock, Texas. Long before megachurches dotted the country, the sanctuary of FBC filled with thousands of Texas Tech college students every Sunday morning at nine thirty. College students, after late Saturday evenings of fun, filled the pews to hear Dan Yeary preach. Why? He had a passion for God, a heart for college students, and a desire to see them connect. The fact that he was an excellent presenter of God's Word who made it relevant to students was evident from the first word out of his mouth. God called and anointed Dan to walk in that good work, which he faithfully did. Blonde, smiling Melinda mirrored Dan's love for the Lord and college students and was by his side. They were a powerful couple for God, and continue to be, as Dan now serves as senior pastor at North Phoenix Baptist church.

In 2009, when I led my P.R.A.Y. with Passion Conference at Dan's church, I planned to see him and Melinda. However, she had an emergency hospitalization while I was there. Since she's unable to work at the computer, Dan graciously corresponded with me regarding her testimony. I wasn't sure Melinda would feel like visiting, since she had recently returned home from a second emergency hospital stay. Dan's comments regarding Melinda and her hospitalizations? "Our Lord blessed us, and she is now home. I have hired two nurses to keep a close watch. Wish you could see her. She's a beautiful testimony, and her sweet spirit is a gift. We've had four hospitalizations this year totaling two months. MS is a formidable disease, but Melinda's spirit and faith have made her a conqueror."

I called Melinda on October 25, 2010. Following is a portion of our conversation during which Christ's Spirit and strength poured through this sweet mother and wife.

Strength in the Midst of Plan B

Debbie: *Melinda, I don't know how you do it.*

Melinda: It isn't easy. Luckily, I didn't have it when Dan was University Minister. I have Progressive MS. The first two years weren't that hard. I could take someone's arm to help me walk.

Debbie: *How old were you when you were diagnosed?*

Melinda: I was thirty-eight. The kids were pretty young. I could still do homeroom activities. One time, though, I went to one of their games and couldn't walk. A friend gave me a piggyback ride to get me to the car. My son saw and said, "Mom! That was so embarrassing." It affected everybody. They started recording the games so I could watch them at home when I couldn't go.

Debbie: *I can't imagine how hard it must have been.*

Melinda: The children and Dan were so sweet. Everyone was supportive. I couldn't have gone through it without Jesus' help.

Debbie: *How does He help you?*

Melinda: I ask Him to help me, and He does. I pray He'll help me in everything; that I'll be an example to people; and for Dan, because this has been hard on him.

Debbie: *How did you find out you had MS?*

Melinda: I was playing tennis and couldn't see the ball. Dan took me to the eye doctor, who then sent me to an eye-care institute. The doctor there looked into my eyes and said, "You have MS." I said, "What's that?" That night we told our children. Doak, our eight-year-old, said, "Mama, are you going to die?" I told him, "We're all going to die some day. But I'm not going to die tomorrow." He said, "Okay," and went to sleep. Dan has really been steady and very helpful.

Debbie: *Were you ever angry at God?*

Melinda: No.

Debbie: *Did you ever ask, "Why me?"*

Melinda: No. I've chosen to think positive. I've always been a positive person. I got that from my mother. I grew up in a positive home. You need to be as positive as you can be. It's important to have a positive Christian witness.

Lessons from a Plan A Mom in a Plan B World

As Melinda and I visited, I couldn't help but note several points we Plan A moms in our Plan B world can take to heart.

1. Check your heart

Melinda is sincere. She isn't fake. She doesn't put a smile on her face while, in her heart, resenting that she can't do things other women do. She acknowledged, "It isn't easy." However, her next words were, "Luckily, I didn't have it when. . . ."

Why is it important to not put a smile on our faces while harboring negative thoughts within? In addition to Jesus seeing our hearts, our children "read" us better than we think. Yes, we may need to put our bodies or minds in a position of praise when we don't feel like it. Our feelings may follow our will. However, if there's a real disconnect between what we truly feel and what we say or the smile we wear, our children will eventually pick up on it. The condition of our heart is central to our relationship with God and our parenting (Matthew 15:19; 22:37).

2. Check your resolve

Melinda chooses to be positive. Instead of bemoaning the years she lost of being able to hop in her car and drive herself to her children's activities, she expressed gratefulness for the years she had to do these things before struck by MS. "I've chosen to think positive," she said. As I thought about her words, I was reminded of the choice we all have. We may be robbed of our health, our spouse may abandon us or die, or we may suffer financial loss. However, no one can rob us of our will and freedom to choose how we respond to life.

The psalmist David expressed this right in Psalm 9:1–2. "I will give thanks to the Lord with all my heart; I will tell of all Your wonders. I will be glad and exult in You; I will sing praise to Your name, O Most High." We can almost hear his resolve and determination when he says, "I will. . . ." I heard the same determination in Melinda's voice.

Children imitate their parents. What resolve do our children hear in our voices? Are we resolved to give thanks to the Lord, to tell of His wonders, to be glad and exult in Him, and sing praises to Him?

3. Check the legacy you're leaving your children

Melinda is passing down a legacy of being positive. When I prodded her about what, besides Jesus (because I know plenty of Christian mothers who are negative), made her tick, she said she learned to be positive from her mother. At that moment it was as though a dagger pierced my heart. I wondered how many opportunities I had missed with Taylor and Lauren to create a more positive home environment. Moms, we can't change the environment in which we were raised. We can't change the past environment in which we raised our children. However, we can begin creating a more positive environment today. Since today—this moment, this breath—is all we have, let's use it and pass down to our children a legacy like Melinda's mother passed down to her.

If you need mentoring on how to develop a more positive attitude, study Melinda's responses. For instance, in addition to expressing gratefulness for the years of health she had before her diagnosis, she was grateful even in the early stages of MS that she could still help with her kids' homeroom activities. How do you feel about your kids' homeroom activities? Do you dread them or view them as an opportunity to get to better know your child's teacher and the students in the class?

Instead of complaining that she had difficulty walking, Melinda expressed gratefulness that she could take someone's arm to help her walk. Are we too focused on our aches and pains and thrown into a tailspin at the slightest discomfort? Or do we take as good care of ourselves as possible, eat healthily, and try to get enough rest so we're not constantly complaining?

James 1:2 calls us to consider it joy when we encounter various trials, knowing that the testing of our faith produces endurance. In Romans 5:3–5 Paul says, "we also exult in our tribulations, knowing that tribulation brings about perseverance; and perseverance, proven character, and proven character, hope; and hope does not disappoint, because the love of God has been poured out within our hearts through the Holy Spirit who was given to us." In these passages we're not told to "be happy" when a Plan B car accident, death, affair, divorce, or illness occurs. Rather, we're reminded that with God on our side and the Holy Spirit in us, our Plan B isn't the end. Sin, illness, and the world don't have the final say in our lives. God has already won the victory. He can and will pour out His love in our hearts when we're in the thick of Plan B. That's what I heard in Melinda's voice. It's what our children need to hear in our voices. It is the legacy we can leave them.

4. Check your alternatives

Moms often get upset if things don't go according to their Plan A. Melinda models finding alternatives when Plan B presents roadblocks. Instead of continuing to embarrass her son by getting piggyback rides to the car, she watched recordings of his games. She didn't whine when telling me this. I, on the other hand, can easily imagine feeling sorry for myself if unable to attend my children's activities.

Jesus is the master model of using Plan B alternatives to accomplish God's will. Early in His ministry, when people turned from "speaking well of Him" (Luke 4:22) to trying to throw Him off a cliff (Luke 4:30), Jesus left Nazareth and went to Capernaum, where He showed His power over demons, disease, and defilement.

Plan B is not the end when we place it in God's hands. Moms, are we modeling for our children how we can look for God's alternative when our Plan A doesn't come through? If Jake doesn't make the soccer team, is it because God wired him to be a golfer? If Marti doesn't make cheerleader, is it because God wants her hours to be spent cheering others to deeper devotion to Christ at Young Life meetings? We can raise our children to look for alternatives when Plan B presents roadblocks.

5. Check your appreciation of and gratitude for others

Melinda appreciates people. Repeatedly she expressed appreciation for her family.

Where are you, on a scale of 1 to 10, in expressing your appreciation to your family? In case you think, "But they don't do anything for me," I'd like to encourage you to consider all you might have for which to be grateful: "I appreciate your calling to let me know you were running late." "I appreciate your helping Mommy." "I appreciate your eating your food so politely." "I appreciate your bringing your plate to the sink and rinsing it." "I appreciate your coming home for the holidays." "I appreciate your picking up milk on the way home."

If our children are short on gratitude, we need look no further than ourselves for someone to blame. Gratitude is something we must teach to and model for our children, even as God's Word teaches gratitude and Jesus models it in the following scriptures:

- "He appointed some of the Levites as ministers before the ark of the Lord, even to celebrate and to *thank and praise* the Lord God of Israel" (1 Chronicles 16:4).

- "Oh *give thanks* to the Lord, call upon His name; make known His deeds among the peoples" (1 Chronicles 16:8).

- "It is good to *give thanks* to the Lord and to sing praises to Your name, O Most High; to declare Your lovingkindness in the morning and Your faithfulness by night" (Psalm 92:1–2).

- "He took the seven loaves and the fish; and *giving thanks*, He broke them and started giving them to the disciples" (Matthew 15:36).

- "When He had taken a cup and *given thanks*, He gave it to them, saying, 'Drink from it, all of you'" (Matthew 26:27).

- "He *rejoiced greatly* in the Holy Spirit, and said, '*I praise You*, O Father, Lord of heaven and earth'" (Luke 10:21).

- "As you have received Christ Jesus the Lord, so walk in Him, having been firmly rooted and now being built up in Him and established in your faith, just as you were instructed, and *overflowing with gratitude*" (Colossians 2:6–7).

- "Since we receive a kingdom which cannot be shaken, let us *show gratitude*, by which we may offer to God an acceptable service with reverence and awe" (Hebrews 12:28).

Are we teaching our children by example to have gratitude to God and others in the midst of Plan B problems, challenges, and illnesses?

6. Check your source of inner strength

"I couldn't go through it without Jesus' help," is at the core of Melinda's success in parenting while having MS. I'd like to add an observation. Unbelievers go through Plan Bs too, and they may "think positive" or not. However, Melinda says that she couldn't maintain her courage, stamina, and sweet spirit without Jesus' help. How does Jesus help? He strengthens her in her inner being (Philippians 4:13). He comforts her (2 Corinthians 1:3–4). As she abides in Him, the strengthening flow of His Holy Spirit runs through her heart and mind, producing love, joy, peace, patience, kindness, goodness, faithfulness, gentleness, and self-control (Galatians 5:22–23). Do your children know that the source of your stamina and fortitude is Jesus?

7. Check your focus

Melinda is others-centered. Rather than being self-absorbed, she continues to serve others, as she has by sharing her testimony with us. In the following paragraphs, you'll read how she continues to try to do as much as possible, sometimes even frustrating her family, who are lovingly concerned for her. She also shared with me how she encouraged another woman with MS to continue to attend church and hear the preaching of God's Word. Although Melinda may not be able to do everything she once did, she continues to find ways to bless others.

We can teach our children the importance of serving others by taking a meal to a family, passing along clothing items to others who might need them, giving a ride to a neighbor who can't drive, or offering encouraging words.

A Legacy of Faith

I also had the opportunity to visit with all three of Dan and Melinda's children. Wes, the oldest, is the Athletics Chaplain at Baylor University. Missy Yeary Wells is a mother of three, works part time, and is married to Steve Wells, who pastors at South Main Baptist Church is Houston. Doak, the youngest Yeary sibling, is a firefighter in Miami, Florida. They shared their insights on their mom and how her struggle with MS has impacted them.

Doak

I was eight when mom was diagnosed with MS, so I saw her change daily; from walking to using a cane, then a walker, and finally a wheelchair. The hardest part was her stubborn will; but it's also what kept her going and being Mom. I learned to iron and do other things earlier than Wes and Missy because I had to. Mom wasn't a quitter, so it taught me not to be a quitter. Never once did she complain or whine. She's an amazing woman who has great faith and love for the Lord. Her having MS has made me more compassionate. I know a man with MS, and he knows he can call me when he falls. Watching them also makes me to want to say to people who complain about minor things, "You should try having MS."

Wes

Mom was diagnosed when I was in high school, so throughout college I watched the change take place in her. After graduating, I returned home and lived with Mom and Dad for five years to help and give back to Mom. The mother I had growing up, who took us everywhere, was different from the mom my younger brother, Doak, had. But Mom's spirit and desire to love and serve us never changed.

I have two outstanding memories. When I would find Mom on the floor, she always apologized that I had to pick her up. I would say, "Mom, you never have to say you're sorry," but she always did. One time, when no one was home, she was sitting on the couch, leaned over, and fell off. When I got home and picked her up, she apologized. I said, "No, mom. I'm sorry you had to be on the floor so long." She answered, "It was fine. I got to pray for all of you all and got in a little nap."

Another time I picked Mom up when I found her at the bottom of the stairs. There was blood on her nose and lip. "Mom, what were you doing?" I asked. "I was taking clean clothes upstairs for you," she said. We tried to take care of those kinds of things, and it frustrated us that Mom tried to do them. But the thing that made her keep trying was also her strength. She battles the disease by saying, "I'm not giving in." Looking back, I appreciate the "fight" my mom has. It's the same fight she now uses as she sits in her wheelchair and attempts to eat with one hand. When food falls, she just smiles and tries to catch it again. She's the toughest person I know.

One significant moment was when she sensed the frustration in my eyes and that I wanted to help her. Since she couldn't move, she said, "Come here. Listen to me, Wes. I can do even MS through Christ who gives me strength."

In Philippians 4:11–13 Paul said, "I found the secret of being content. I can do all things through Christ who gives me strength." Mom became a living example of those verses. I share that with students all the time. It's what encourages me so often. Also, my parents' example of a godly marriage has been phenomenal; watching Mom and Dad go through this and seeing how they've loved and served each other through it—I can't imagine a greater example.

When I think of Mom, I think of strength, a fighter. Most people wouldn't envision a fighter as someone who can't move. But Mom has never had a bad day. She's shed a tear here or there, but she always says she's fine. She says, "You know we've prayed for healing. I know I'll be healed. I just don't know when: in this life or when God gives me a new body."

Mom lives with confidence that God will see her through. So when we're putting her in the car and hit her head on the roof, she just laughs. Or if her shoe falls off, she laughs. It's phenomenal that she's not bitter. I can't explain it outside of her dependency on Christ.

Mom doesn't let things discourage her. That comes from her hope and trust in Christ. There's peace knowing she's in His hands. When she got MS, I saw in action what I had heard her say about her faith. When Mom and Dad were put to the test, they said, "This is where we trust the Lord." Even when they didn't understand, they didn't waver or doubt. They humbly trusted and said, "We'll keep walking through this together."

It has been amazing to have someone not just say, "This is what we believe," but to see it in action. Mom's legacy of faith is invaluable to us.

Missy

Even when mom was first diagnosed, there was never a sense of fear. She and Dad said, "We're going to take this one day at a time." She was the same mom she had always been. She still encouraged us, and our house still had a revolving door—it was still a place where friends gathered. She loved to play hostess and was constantly feeding everybody. We never felt like we couldn't bring a load of friends to hang out in the den, and she was at the center of it; always sharing her faith from the inside out. She never let what was happening with her body affect her spirit. Even to this day, when her body has been ravaged, she tells people about Jesus and invites them to church. She's an incredible inspiration.

Power from Jesus to You

Dan said, "MS is a formidable disease, but Melinda's spirit and faith have made her a conqueror." In the thirty minutes I visited with Melinda on the phone, I was deeply touched by her strong spirit. Although she easily tires, she was determined to talk with me. She wanted her testimony to be of help to you.

In Psalm 121:1 the psalmist asks, "From whence shall my help come?" Then he answers as Melinda did: "My help comes from the Lord." When we think about our Plan B mothering challenges, we may feel overwhelmed. But when we consider our God and Helper, the One who made the heavens and earth, it puts things in perspective.

With what God-sized mothering problem are you confronted? Are you at your wits' end with a strong-willed child? Are your emotions controlling you instead of you controlling them in relation to your teen? Are you worried sick over your adult child? Whatever your Plan B situation, I pray you're encouraged by Melinda's testimony. Jesus' strengthening power is available to you, too, as we'll see in this next biblical illustration.

The account of the woman with an issue of blood has fascinated me since I studied her when writing *If God is In Control, Why Do I have a Headache?*[1] Both Mark and Luke note that Jesus perceived power going out from Him to the woman. Mark 5:29–30 states, "Immediately the flow of her blood was dried up; and she felt in her body that she was healed of her affliction. Immediately Jesus, perceiving in Himself that the power proceeding from Him had gone forth, turned around in the crowd and said, 'Who touched My garments?'"

Plan A Mom Tip

Rely on Christ's strength and empowerment rather than focusing on your weakness.

Four points stand out in this passage. First, Jesus has the power you need. Second, in faith you can reach out and touch Him in prayer. Third, Jesus is aware when you pray, and His power proceeds to you. Fourth, there are many people "around" Jesus, but His power goes only to those who reach out to Him in faith.

---※---

LIVE OUT LOUD

Plan A Mom Checkup

1. Are you simply a member of the crowd at your church or a daily recipient of Jesus' power?
2. When things don't go as you like, would your family say you tend to be more negative or positive?
3. What legacy are you leaving your children? A legacy of worry? A legacy of self-absorption? Or the legacy, "I can do all things through Christ who strengthens me?"
4. What positive effect would it have on your children if you became more loving, kind, unselfish, grateful, and hopeful?
5. Ask God to strengthen you and give you a more positive attitude of praise and appreciation for Him and others. Pray that your children observe the change in you and follow your example.

LOVE OUT LOUD

1. What is significant to you about the woman with the issue of blood?
2. What spoke to your heart in the comments from Melinda's family about how she faces her Plan B illness?
3. Melinda's story shows us that no matter what Plan B we experience, our children can learn and benefit from our attitude. Which of the points under "Lessons from a Plan A Mom in a Plan B World" most challenges you? Why? Which do you want to incorporate into your life?
4. Which of the following scriptures will you memorize to help you when faced with a Plan B?
    ☐ "I can do all things through Christ who strengthens me" (Philippians 4:13).

- □ "I'll give thanks to the Lord with all my heart; I'll tell of all Your wonders. I'll be glad and exult in You; I'll sing praise to Your name, O Most High" (Psalm 9:1–2).
- □ "God is our refuge and strength, a very present help in trouble" (Psalm 46:1).

Between You and God—Principle to Remember

I defuse the land mine of focusing
on my weakness by asking Jesus to help me.

Father, thank You that Your power proceeds from You to me when I reach out to You in faith and prayer. Help me model for my children living by Your power and with an attitude of gratitude. In Jesus' name, amen.

Laugh Out Loud

One morning, when Taylor was a tiny tyke, he walked into the kitchen, looked up at me, and with a serious expression asked, "How does God get dinosaurs to heaven?" I suppose my blank stare and lack of a ready answer prompted his clarification: "Well, they're so heavy." Isn't it wonderful that children don't question God's strength and ability—they're just curious how He'll show it.

16

DANGEROUS ISOLATION OR SUPPORTIVE FRIENDSHIP

I defuse the land mine of isolation by
developing prayerful and supportive friendships.

If one can overpower him who is alone, two can resist him.
A cord of three strands is not quickly torn apart.

Ecclesiastes 4:12

Looking in the mirror, I wondered at the woman staring back at me. Tousled hair, a new set of wrinkles, red eyes, haggard. She looked like a train had run over her. Doing a double take, I checked. Yes, it was me.

Have you ever woken, looked in the mirror, and wanted to gasp, "Who is that person?!" If not, trust me, one day you will. Motherhood and time have a way of doing that to you. Some days are easier than others. Some moments are easier, such as when your little angels are asleep. The truth is, though, once you have a baby, your life is never the same. Even if baby number one is perfect, seldom will baby number two nap at the same time. Between feeding, bathing, teething, potty training, washing, cooking, cleaning, rocking, telling bedtime stories, grocery shopping, paying the bills, baking cookies for school parties, ironing, vacuuming, sweeping, feeding the dog, making the beds, changing crib sheets, and making trips to the doctor, dentist, and candlestick maker (oops, how did that one slip in?), there's little time for Mommy.

Add to the mix in-laws, teachers, coaches, friends, enemies, church activities, after-school activities, fund-raisers, and the ridiculous numbers of papers you have to sign per child at the beginning of each school year, and it makes you wonder if you're really cut out to be a mommy.

My sweet daughter, who has a very active toddler and is pregnant with child number two, recently commented that she would be glad when she got through the first trimester and was no longer so tired. After making the same comment a number of times, I finally burst her bubble. "Lauren, get used to it. You're a mother. You'll be tired the rest of your life." Thank goodness, my daughter has a sense of humor and laughed with me. However, motherhood unquestionably requires more hours of the day and night than any other job. It taxes you physically, emotionally, psychologically, mentally, financially, and spiritually. Add any more demands, and it's easy to understand why many moms struggle with, depression, or perhaps turning inward, finding it too difficult to maintain friendships—especially if others are critical of our children or parenting.

Such was the case with a dear friend of mine. However, she has a good word for us about the importance of Christian friends, surrender, and the power of God.

When you get the word you're pregnant, the feeling of your child's potential fills your heart. You love your baby instantly and with everything you are.

At one of my baby showers, a group of women surrounded me to pray for the little girl growing in my womb. One woman prayed, "Lord fill her even now with your Holy Spirit to be anointed to serve and honor You. Give her the ability to hide Your Word in her heart." As she spoke, the baby went crazy with movement! Even before her birth, we knew God had a plan for her life.

Once she arrived, she was a delight and joy, always filling the room with singing; extremely intelligent, independent, and determined to do whatever she set out to do.

Around the age of two, however, she started to have bizarre, out-of-the-blue fits of rage. She'd be happy one moment and suddenly become angry for no reason. At first my husband and I believed it to be a bad case of the terrible twos, but then we began noticing other behavior that led us to believe we might have a much more serious issue. For one thing, she always had to be moving. She would rock back and forth or bang her head against the wall or on the floor. She bit, hit, and pinched the kids in the nursery. Every Sunday I had to prepare myself to be pulled from the service to calm her. More and more often, I had to take her home or walk her while my husband finished the service. For a season I quit going.

As the years went on, these episodes escalated. She would try to hurt herself and others. She would trash her room in a rage, throw and break things.

After having other children and seeking professional counsel, we began to realize our now five-year-olds' problems weren't due to our parenting skills or lack of—although "friends" and family often told us it was. (Always nice to have someone on the outside looking in and passing judgment.) We saw several doctors, who informed us our daughter had a genius IQ, severe attention deficit/hyperactivity disorder, and bipolar disorder. I still remember the day the doctor said those words. I was glad to finally have some answers, but I was devastated. I began reading everything I could on those topics. Yet learning what our future held in light of her disorder was overwhelming.

It's been a long and difficult journey that has affected not only us as parents but also her siblings, who would grow silent or retreat to their rooms when our daughter had a fit. Their fear was they would get hurt—and it was a realistic fear.

It's heartbreaking to have to learn how to restrain your child in a "safety hold" so she can't hurt you and others while in her rage. Sometimes the need to restrain her continued so long that I couldn't sustain my hold and my husband would have to take over. Having a child with a mental disorder is physically, emotionally, and spiritually exhausting. Our days were filled with despair.

We had to pull her from pre-K and private school twice. Parents and teachers withdrew from us and talked about us behind our backs. Yes, even the body of believers can be hurtful. We made a life change, and I homeschooled, which was a bad idea. It began to destroy what little relationship I had with my daughter. After one semester, we hired someone to come to our home and teach. It made us feel so vulnerable for her to see the ugliness of the disorder up close, day in and day out. Sometimes our daughter's manic cycles would last for hours.

I began to withdraw and hid away for years. Only a couple of really close friends had any idea what we were going through, and we limited even what we allowed them to know. We so wanted to protect our child. We felt so alone, always crying out to the Lord: Why her? Why us? Why this pain for our other children? I knew in my heart He had a plan, but could this be it? What purpose did it serve?

I'll never forget the day when the washing machine door broke. It sent me over the edge. I sat in the pile of laundry while my sister tried to console me over the phone. I dropped the phone and the next thing I knew, my daughter's teacher was calling my husband to come home, which he hurriedly did.

The next few days are a blur. My husband called an aunt to take our daughter for the week. Then he did the best thing he could have done: he rallied the troops. He called our close friends and spilled the awful details and was VERY transparent. He asked them to pray. Our friends became to us as Aaron and Hur were to Moses when they held up his arms in battle (Exodus 17:11–13).

No longer did we isolate ourselves after seeing where isolation got us! Although that period was our most difficult time, it also was a turning point—a complete release of our daughter and her future to our Lord. With the help and counsel of friends and doctors, we began to move forward again. We found a certified teacher who wanted to teach her. This was the beginning of healing for our daughter and our family. She began to thrive! Her teacher and family loved her and prayed for her. Prayer was always their first line of defense. Another lesson: when you're too tired even to pray, get someone else to pray!

We began to feel God telling us to take her off her medicines, which we did against the doctor's wishes. We needed to regroup and assess where she was. Changing medicines can really mess up a child, so we just wanted to start over. Within three weeks of coming off meds, we noticed a huge change in her for the better. Within six weeks, I felt I had my "real" daughter for the first time in years.

God had healed her! She now attends public school, and she is thriving. She loves the Lord and is a leader to her peers. She knows God's Word, and God has given her an amazing ability to hide it in her heart. I know she's anointed to serve and honor Him. She always has a song on her lips; her voice fills our home on a daily basis.

Remember the prayer for her at my shower? Although we still sometimes see the ADHD, our daughter is in every way a delight and joy to be around.

I have tears as I write this, just thinking back to where we were and how far God has brought us. We have a BIG GOD! My friends often hear me quote this verse: "Not by might, nor by power, but by My Spirit, says the Lord" (Zechariah 4:6).

The Danger of Isolation and the Value of Christian Friends

Isolation is dangerous, whether you're a captured soldier in a distant land or a mom in your own home. When we're isolated from others, our perspective can become skewed. It's easy for our imaginations to run wild and for us to think the worst about ourselves, our children, and the future. Hopelessness can settle in. While the Bible recommends time alone with God, it never suggests we pull away from the community of faith. Rather, God's Word encourages and demonstrates the importance of Christian friends.

The Value of Christian Friends for Fellowship and Ministry

Jesus was busier and more taxed than any of us can imagine. Yet He placed great value on friendships. We find Him in the home of Mary and Martha, having dinner with His good friend Lazarus. He considered the disciples His friends . . . including Judas, whom He still called "friend" on the night he betrayed Jesus (Matthew 26:50).

Will our friends sometimes fail us or disappoint us? Might we be betrayed by a friend? Yes. But that's not enough reason for us to withdraw from all friends. Proverbs 27:10 tells us, "Do not forsake your own friend or your father's friend, and do not go to your brother's house in the day of your calamity; better is a neighbor who is near than a brother far away." Proverbs 27:9 affirms the value of friends and their counsel: "Oil and perfume make the heart glad, so a man's counsel is sweet to his friend."

We may look with some envy at others who seem to have lots of friends. However, Proverbs 18:24 teaches us the value of even one good friend: "A man of too many friends comes to ruin, but there is a friend who sticks closer than a brother."

Friends are important because, without a doubt, there will be times when we need to be ministered to, as was the woman in the testimony above and even the great apostle Paul: "He gave orders to the centurion for him [Paul] to be kept in custody and yet have some freedom, and not to prevent any of his friends from ministering to him" (Acts 24:23).

The Value of Christian Friends for Discipleship

Throughout the Bible we read of people gathering for discipleship. Jesus gathered twelve men and discipled them for three years. Later, people gathered in homes to be taught by those disciples. Paul stayed with Priscilla and Aquila while he was in

Corinth and worked with them as a tent maker. Cornelius called together not only relatives but also close friends to hear Peter teach about Jesus (Acts 10:24).

Some of Jesus' last words were a mandate for us to make disciples and teach others all that He had taught (Matthew 28:19–20). In a discipleship setting, we can study God's principles that affect our parenting, such as a book like this one explores.

The Value of Christian Friends for Prayer

While Jesus taught the importance of individual, private prayer and not praying for show (Matthew 6:5–7), He also taught the value of friends praying together. When the disciples were gathered with Jesus, one of the first things He taught them was to pray (Matthew 6:7–15). He took Peter and John with Him to the Mount of Transfiguration. There God emphasized the importance of not just talking but also listening to Jesus.

Jesus took His friends with Him to the Garden of Gethsemane in His time of deepest need and prayer. He asked them to keep watch with Him (Matthew 26:36–38).

Jesus emphasized the value praying with one or two friends: "Truly I say to you, whatever you bind on earth shall have been bound in heaven; and whatever you loose on earth shall have been loosed in heaven. Again I say to you, that if two of you agree on earth about anything that they may ask, it shall be done for them by My Father who is in heaven. For where two or three have gathered together in My name, I am there in their midst" (Matthew 18:18–20).

How much clearer can Jesus be on the value of prayer with friends?

The Value of Christian Friends for Accountability

Sometimes our thinking can become unclear. In our world of changing diapers, doing the wash, driving carpool, and herding teenagers, we can fall into negative thinking, self-abasing attitudes, worldly practices, or poor parenting habits. We may have thought we'd never yell at out kids but find ourselves screaming "NO! I said NO!" across the room and over the noise of the DVD player, all to no avail. We may have promised ourselves we wouldn't let our kids eat junk food, only to one day realize they haven't had a green bean since . . . well, we can't remember. We may have said if we ever caught our teen drinking, we'd take away the car keys; but we've gone soft. We may have been committed to attending church, but with the family's busy weekdays, Sunday has turned into lounge-lizard day.

Enter Christian friends. We need someone who will say, "How's the yelling? Are you turning off the television and looking Becky in the eye when you tell her to clean her room?" We need someone to ask, "What's in your Starbuck's cup? That doesn't smell like coffee." We need someone to insist, "You need more sleep. Let's talk." We need a friend who knows our moods and can say, "What's going on? I can tell you're stressed." We need to know we can pick up the phone and say, "I need you to pray for me. I'm so down" or, "I have this bad habit and can't break it. Would you pray for me?" We need someone with whom it's safe to confess, "I'm losing my temper too much. I'm afraid I may hurt my children."

Pulling away from others won't help you. Christian friends with whom you can talk, study, and pray and who will hold you accountable are God-given blessings. They are one way we can experience "Not by might, nor by power, but by My Spirit, says the Lord" (Zechariah 4:6).

Look in the mirror. What do you see? Rather than shrinking back in seclusion, how about calling a Christian friend for some fellowship and support?

Plan A Mom Tip

Defuse the land mine of dangerous isolation by seeking refuge in friends' prayers and God's power.

LIVE OUT LOUD

Plan A Mom Checkup

1. Have you in the past, or are you now, retreating into isolation? Why?
2. What value do you think there might be in having someone (in addition to Jesus) to talk to?
3. What's keeping you from developing a friendship?
4. If you feel like you don't have anyone you would call "friend" and in whom you could confide, ask God to bring a person into your life to be your friend and to whom you can be a friend. Make a list of people with whom you were once friends but have lost touch. Choose one or two and call them: admit that you've been consumed with kids but would love to have coffee or meet

in the carpool line a few minutes early to catch up. Develop a friendship with a mom whose child is in your child's class. Join a play group or MOPS (Mothers of Preschoolers). Start attending church again. If you're single, ask someone if she would mind your sitting with her for the worship service or Bible class.

5. Pray and thank God for being your friend, for never leaving you or forsaking you.

LOVE OUT LOUD

1. Which is easier for you: to withdraw or to develop and maintain friendships?
2. Share tips for developing and maintaining friendships.
3. What dangers do you see in pulling away from friends when you're struggling with a difficult parenting issue?
4. If you have an accountability partner, how does that relationship work?
5. What value is there in studying God's Word together in a discipleship format?
6. What can you apply to your own life from the testimony of the mother in this chapter?
7. What value is there in having an Aaron or Hur to pray with you about parenting matters?
8. What passage of Scripture used in this chapter is meaningful to you? Why?

BETWEEN YOU AND GOD—PRINCIPLE TO REMEMBER

I defuse the land mine of isolation by
developing prayerful and supportive friendships.

Father, thank You that You created us to live in fellowship with one another. I don't have to handle my problems alone. Thank You for prayer, by which I can enter Your presence and receive help and empowerment to be a better parent. Please help me to develop friendships that honor You and that help me be a better mother. In Jesus' name, amen.

LAUGH OUT LOUD

We were driving home from Lubbock through the countryside one night, and Daniel looked up at the sky and asked, "Where are all those airplanes going?" Living in Dallas, he'd never seen that many stars—he thought every one of them was an airplane.—Pam Couch

17

ANGRY AND CONFUSED OR OF A SOUND MIND

I defuse the land mine of "mommy meltdowns" by keeping
my mind focused on Christ and His plans for my life.

*We are His workmanship, created in Christ Jesus for good works, which
God prepared beforehand so that we would walk in them.*

Ephesians 2:10

Many things can cause moms to feel angry and confused. I recently had
a little "meltdown" and would love nothing more than to blame it on hormones.
Poor Keith. I began the morning as devout Debbie and ended the day as the wicked
witch of the West. Let's face it: as much as we try to be good mommies, we're going
to stumble and fall at times. That's why our daily Christian experience is referred to
in the Bible as a walk. As God's children, we're learning to walk as citizens of heaven
while still living in a Plan B world. We hope that most of the time we're stepping out
on the right foot—the one grounded in biblical principles and God's love.

   One woman in the Bible who ranks high on the angry and confused mom list is
Zipporah, Moses' wife. As you recall, Moses fled to Midian after killing an Egyptian
taskmaster. Zipporah first laid eyes on Moses at a well where she and her sisters were
watering their father's sheep. When some shepherds came and drove the flock away,
Moses came to the rescue and watered the sheep. Now, isn't he a nice guy? Attentive

to Zipporah's needs. Rescuing her from hard work and unkind shepherds. Putting her first.

When the sisters returned home early that day, they explained, "An Egyptian delivered us from the hand of shepherds, and what is more, he even drew the water for us and watered the flock" (Exodus 2:19).

Moses, this handsome hunk, must have looked pretty good to these seven sisters. Plus, he was thoughtful and kind. Exodus 2:21 says, "Moses was willing to dwell with the man [the girls' father], and he gave his daughter Zipporah to Moses. Then she gave birth to a son, and he named him Gershom."

So Zipporah is married to a wonderful, thoughtful, handsome man, and they have a baby. She's living near her family. Life is great. Then God interrupts her perfectly happy life. While she's been playing house in Midian, the Hebrew people, enslaved in Egypt, have been crying out to God for deliverance. God heard their groanings and set a bush on fire in Midian to get Moses' attention.

When we put ourselves in Zipporah's sandals for a moment, we're better able to grasp why, a few chapters later, she has a meltdown. One morning her husband of forty or so years leaves for work. He comes home a different man. He says God talked to him through a burning bush and told him to return to Egypt. "Start packing. Get the children's things. God wants us to leave immediately."

Zipporah probably stared at Moses, wondering what in the world had happened to him. Heat stroke, maybe? Moses continues: "God has called me to deliver the Hebrew people out of Egyptian bondage. I'm going to turn my staff into a serpent as proof to Pharaoh."

No doubt Zipporah is now horrified. "What if Pharaoh doesn't believe you, Moses?" she likely asked. Moses is quick to answer, "God told me to turn the Nile River into blood."

We jump to Exodus 4:20, where Moses is en route with his family to Egypt. On the way, however, things heat up. Moses hadn't fulfilled the Hebrew covenant of circumcising his son Gershom: a significant violation of God's laws. Verse 24 tells us that "the Lord met him [Moses] at the lodge and sought to put him to death."

Now the scene switches to Zipporah. She's in a strange place. She probably doesn't want to be on this journey. Most likely, she thinks her husband has gone off the deep end and is having a midlife crisis. She's not happy about moving away from her family. And now Moses' God, who called them on this venture, is going to kill him because Gershom isn't circumcised. Madder than a hornet and not wanting to be stuck in Egypt with a dead husband and two little boys, she grabs a knife and removes Gershom's foreskin, then throws it at Moses. Yes, that's right. In case you don't believe me, Exodus 4:25 records it: "Zipporah took a flint and cut off her son's foreskin and threw it at Moses' feet, and she said, 'You are indeed a bridegroom of blood to me.'" I imagine Gershom was screaming at the top of his lungs, son number two was hiding, and Moses, lying on his deathbed, was too weak to remove the bloody foreskin from his feet. This is not a pretty sight. And you thought you'd had a bad day.

Losing It or Finding It

Most of us can probably sympathize a bit with Zipporah. The Bible doesn't give us any indication that God confirmed to her in a dream that He had indeed called Moses to be the deliverer. Zipporah had to totally rely on Moses and that what he claimed was true. And it was a wild story.

Can you relate on any level? Perhaps your husband has left you, and you feel alone and scared. You may not have flung a body part, but perhaps you've thrown a pillow or two across the room during your little meltdown. Or you may be married and scared to death because your husband is walking away from a perfectly stable job, and moving you and your kids to an unfamiliar place to start a new business. He says God told him to, but God hasn't told you. Or maybe you're close to "losing it" because your children's father is sick or dying. You've prayed and asked God to spare him, but to no avail. You may be fearful at the prospect of a Plan B widowhood and not knowing how you'll raise your children. You may be in a second marriage with stepchildren who want nothing to do with you. You've hung on so far, but you don't think you can take it much longer.

Mommy meltdowns happen to all of us sooner or later. Whether they're due to fluctuating hormones, anger, or fear, God doesn't want us to stay in that state. He doesn't want us to "lose it" and not "find it." He wants us to find Him—our Rescuer, Deliverer, Hope, and Help—and to find Him sufficient to meet our every need.

Shortly after the foreskin episode, in which both Moses and Zipporah learned that God is to be honored and obeyed, God sent Aaron, Moses' brother, to meet him in the wilderness. Moses and Aaron then assembled all the elders and sons of Israel and shared with them what God had said. Moses then performed miraculous signs in the sight of the people as proof. The people believed and were grateful that God had heard their cries. Exodus 4:31 says they bowed low and worshipped.

Owning Our Emotions and Mental State

Something huge was happening in the lives of the people of three nations: Midian, Egypt, and Israel. The Midianite wife didn't seem to get it. The Hebrews got it. The Egyptians were soon to get it, whether they wanted to or not. Zipporah may not have initially understood what was happening, but then she had every opportunity to see and believe, just as Moses, Aaron, and the Hebrews did. She had the opportunity to be a part of what God was doing, to encourage her husband, and allow her children to participate. But she didn't. Exodus 18:2 tells us that instead, Moses sent her and her sons back home to her father.

Herbert Lockyer, in *All the Women of the Bible*, notes the following about Zipporah: "She disappears without comment from the history of the Jewish people in which her husband figured so prominently. 'Neither as the wife of her husband nor as the mother of her children did she leave behind her a legacy of spiritual riches.'"[1] Zipporah will forever remain the angry woman who threw her son's foreskin at Moses' feet and hissed, "You are indeed a bridegroom of blood to me." That's the image. Those are her only recorded words.

There will be times we don't act or talk like Jesus. God knows that. We know that. Our spouse and children know that. No one expects perfection this side of heaven. However, we are responsible for our emotional and mental state. Just as we lovingly forgive our children when they act or speak in unbecoming ways, so God forgives us. And just as we expect our children to behave according to their age and maturity, God expects us to also.

Have you been a Christian for a long time? Are you better at handling your emotions than when you first came to Christ? What about your thoughts? Do you more often obediently guard what you allow to come into your mind and quickly dismiss unbecoming, uninvited thoughts than when you first came to Christ?

What about your self-control? Are you better able to control your body and tongue than you did three years ago? As we look for growth and maturity in our children, so God looks for it in us. If we don't mature, we'll be like Zipporah: out of control, throwing fits, having meltdowns, saying things we regret, and affecting our children in less than God-honoring ways.

Factors that Contribute to Meltdowns

All kinds of factors contribute to mommy meltdowns. Some of them can be prevented.

Marrying Someone You Don't Respect

When we marry, we enter into a one-body covenant with the other person. It's not a contract with a clause that says if our relationship gets worse, someone gets sick, or the money runs out, we leave. Rather, before God, "a man shall leave his father and mother, and be joined to his wife; and they shall become one flesh" (Genesis 2:24). In order to sustain a marriage through bad times, illness, and poverty, God must be a part of the relationship. God can use the rough times and the rough edges of our spouse to produce in us a deeper prayer life and greater intimacy with Him.

Zipporah was happy marrying into the fairy tale of the tall, dark, and handsome Egyptian who would take care of her forever in Midian. However, when God called Moses to a new place, it upset her apple cart. She wanted no part of the Hebrew or God's calling on his life. As a result of her selfishness, their children didn't get to experience the great works God did through their father.

What about your marriage and children? Have you married a man who is a follower of Jesus not just in word but in deed? If so, you're blessed. But are you willing to follow the vision God gives him if it's different from your Plan A?

If you're not married to a follower of Jesus, ask God to awaken within your husband a hunger for God. Pray he will be drawn to Christ in you.

If you're married to a man who says he is a Christian but doesn't read his Bible, pray, or love Christ deeply, pray that he'll be drawn into a more passionate relationship with Christ. Take great care that your husband sees God's Spirit of patience, joy, and love in you.

If you're married to a Christian, pray for your husband's purity, devotion to Christ, hunger for God's Word, and wisdom. Then, when he feels led to do something, you don't have to have a mommy meltdown. You can trust that the sovereign Lord is doing something in your husband's life. Plus, your children will be blessed and have the opportunity to see God at work in your family.

Spreading Yourself Too Thin

Another reason I think moms are often angry and confused and not of sound mind is because of an overcrowded schedule and too many commitments to things God never intended for us to do. When we do everything we and every member of our family wants to do, and everything every teacher, coach, pastor, in-law, coworker, volunteer organization, ministry, and friend wants us to do, we can't help but feel overwhelmed and frustrated—as do our children.

We aren't meant to run nonstop. God and Jesus both modeled resting. Because rest is so important to our functioning correctly, God made it a commandment. Yet we often run as hard and long on Sunday, the day He set aside for rest, as we do every other day of the week. In case you hadn't noticed, God also made day and night. However, with the convenience of electricity, we have circumvented normal work and sleep hours. But is a long-term lifestyle of burning the candle at both ends healthy? Or will lack of mental, physical, and emotional rest contribute to our being stressed-out mom raising stressed-out kids?

Ephesians 2:10 teaches that God has prepared good works for us to do—not every work every person asks us to do. If we aren't discerning, we may commit to too many things and only apply ourselves halfheartedly to the good works to which God called us. Or we may miss God's designated good works altogether. This isn't what God wants for us, and it isn't what He wants us to model for our children.

How do you know if you're overbooked and not effectively doing the good works to which God has called you? Here are some possible warning signs:

- You don't have time to pray.
- You mean to read your Bible but don't get around to it.
- You're easily angered.
- You feel tired all the time.
- You're stressed, irritable, impatient.
- You increasingly find yourself in conflict with others.
- You seldom smile. Life is serious. You feel you have to keep juggling all the balls in the air, or they'll drop.
- You work hard but never feel like you catch up.
- You feel guilty for not being a better mother.

- Your children are irritable, tired, and always busy.
- Your family lives on processed or fast food because you don't have time to cook.
- Your family seldom eats together.

When I asked my Christian friends about the issue of being stretched too thin, one friend said, "I struggle with it all the time. There are only so many hours in the day, and it's impossible to do even half of what I'm asked to do. Being a people pleaser can get me into being overcommitted real fast."

What's the solution? Nicki Carlson, mother of three, tells us what she does: "I take my calendar before the Lord and pray about commitments. It's about discernment. As a faithful Christian and busy mom, if I truly feel God is asking me to do something new and I already have a full calendar, then I know there's another thing God is moving me away from. So, for instance, if you feel strongly that you're supposed to lead a new Bible study, then what do you need to drop?" She also offers this thought: "It's wrong to expect the youngest child to keep up with the whole family. We didn't expect that of the first child. It's a tool of the devil to make us feel we have to do it all. God tells us to be still."

Not Caring Properly for Our Bodies

Along with the danger of being overscheduled is the problem of not selecting foods and drinks that will build up our bodies, which the Bible describes as God's temple (1 Corinthians 6:19–20). One day I woke up and realized that if I didn't pump my body full of caffeine, I couldn't fulfill my commitments. My body would require that I either take a nap or go to bed earlier in the evenings. It didn't take God's voice in a burning bush for me to realize I needed to make a change. God didn't create us to run nonstop. He wired us to sleep and give our bodies and minds rest. Yet with elements like caffeine or even pharmaceutical products, we defy God's laws of nature. Rather than listen to our bodies and respond with God-given common sense, we push ahead, fueled by chemically infused drinks, foods, and pills that can contribute to our being edgy.

At some point, we must stop and evaluate whether our lifestyle is harmful to our children's and our mental, physical, spiritual, and emotional health.

Expecting Perfection

Some meltdowns may be because of our own perfectionism. We not only place high demands on ourselves but also on our children and others.

Demands on Ourselves

I can't help but wonder if we wouldn't be less stressed if women's magazines didn't exist. In my mom's day, holidays consisted of the family gathering and eating yummy food around the table. Thanks to Martha Stewart, if we don't have fresh-flower place cards and serve vegetables from our organic garden that we work in every day before rearranging our linen closet so the sheets have the right crease, then we aren't serving a decent meal in a well-organized, perfectly decorated home.

And we're not supposed to look like regular shaped women who have borne children. Hearing, "Oh, you're so tiny, you don't look like you've even had kids" may make a mom beam—not that I would know. I do know we can put too much emphasis on our outer appearance to the detriment of the inner, hidden person of the heart. Our weight and appearance should be managed for health purposes and to honor God, not to compete with the skinny model on the cover of Cosmo. Let's keep a close check to make sure we're not running ourselves ragged to maintain a certain appearance. Rather, let us follow the advice 1 Peter 3:3–4 gives us: "Your adornment must not be *merely* external—braiding the hair, and wearing gold jewelry, or putting on dresses; but *let it be the hidden person of the heart*, with the imperishable quality of a gentle and quiet spirit, which is precious in the sight of God" (emphasis mine).

Demands on Our Children

Meltdowns can even happen over the red striped shorts worn with the pink and yellow polka-dotted shirt on picture day. Yes, the uncombed hair, saggy jeans, short skirt, nose ring, or whatever, can be less than desirable. Certainly, modesty is a must. However, when your toddler wants to combine stripes and plaids, it may serve you and your child best to put a smile on your face and announce to the workers at Mother's Day Out, "Danny picked out his clothes all by himself!" They'll understand.

Demands on our children to play sports or participate in activities they care nothing about can cause meltdowns too. Taylor had one when he was three. Our church had a wonderful children's choir program and kicked off the year with a party. I knew Taylor would love it. When I took him, though, he wanted nothing to do with it. I showed him the balloons; the teachers tried bribing him with cookies. He cried. I pointed out his friends who were there; you would have thought I was trying to feed him to lions. Frustrated that he wouldn't cooperate, I finally gave up, and we returned home. That was the first of many things Keith and I thought Taylor would want to do but didn't. It was the beginning of our learning what it meant to "train up a child in the way he should go" (Proverbs 22:6). Charles Ryrie comments on this verse: "*Train* may include the idea of dedicate as well as educate. *In the way he should go*, . . . literally means according to his way; i.e., the child's habits and interests. The instruction must take into account his individuality and inclinations and be in keeping with his degree of physical and mental development."

Why do some kids want to join every club and activity and others don't? I don't know. I do know you can't put a square peg in a round hole, and if you try, you'll only frustrate yourself and harm the peg. Sure, encourage activities. If you are determined that your child should play a sport or musical instrument or serve in some capacity, give him or her choices: "Would you prefer piano or guitar lessons?" "Do you want to be in the debate or Spanish club?" "Do you want to be on the Mexico or Kentucky mission team?" Don't force your children to be little replicas of you or to be who you wish they were. Prayerfully watch and listen to your children. Appreciate them for the unique people God created them to be. It's okay to tell your friends, "No, Taylor isn't going to be in debate or on the mock trial team," even though his daddy is the coach. Somehow Taylor turned out. He's a wonderful Christian, loves music, and is practicing law . . . all without preschool church choir and high-school mock trial. Imagine!

Too Much Stuff

Another factor that contributes to mommy meltdowns is having too much stuff. It took me years to learn to not save magazines or every paper and picture my child brought home from school, and that I really don't need tons of towels, sheets, or panties. I mean, how many can you use or wear at one time? Fewer of everything means smaller, more manageable loads to wash and put away and drawers and closets that aren't overflowing. The same goes for toys. Throw away. Give away. Just say no to buying more. "Do not store up for yourselves treasures on earth, where moth and rust destroy, and where thieves break in and steal" (Matthew 6:19).

Disorganization

I hope you have more organizational skills than I did as a young mother. If not, here's a great way to start. At minimum, get two file folders for each child. Label one the child's name, the year, and "Medical." Label the second with the child's name, year, and "Keepsakes." Then, rather than let a stack of papers pile up, drop the items into the file folders when you walk in the door from the doctor or after you've bragged on the school keepsake.

Try to touch things only once. In other words, instead of bringing in the mail and tossing it on the table, then moving it to the counter, to your purse, to the bedroom, deal with it immediately. Junk mail: trash. Outer envelope of bill: trash. Bill: in the "To Pay" file folder. Towels: out of the dryer and folded—don't put them on the couch. Walk them into the bathroom and put them away immediately. You'll be amazed how the little things add up to a happier you. "There is an appointed time for everything. And there is a time for every event under heaven. . . . a time to keep and a time to throw away" (Ecclesiastes 3:1, 6).

Plan A Mom Tip

Eliminate factors
that contribute to
meltdowns. Pray before
accepting commitments.

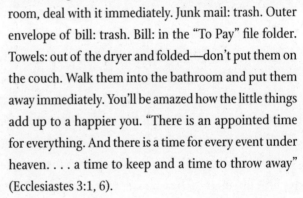

LIVE OUT LOUD

Plan A Mom Checkup

1. Are you frequently an angry and confused meltdown mama? What factors do you think contribute to this?
2. Are you a perfectionist who demands your children be perfect, as defined by your expectations?
3. Do you tend to do everything everyone asks of you? Are you afraid of your children not being a part of or missing something?
4. Are you willing to pray for your husband and do things you might otherwise not do, simply because you respect and pray for him and trust God to lead him?

5. Could part of your and your children's irritability be because your family is overscheduled?

6. Is caffeine a key component of your day and a regular part of your children's diet? What would happen if you cut the caffeine?

7. Discuss your schedules with your children, and pray together for God's wisdom in which activities you and your children should be committed. Discuss Ephesians 2:10 with them.

LOVE OUT LOUD

1. Imagine all the miracles Zipporah and her children missed. If you had been friends with her, how would you have advised her?

2. How might God be speaking to you about your relationship with your husband and children?

3. With which can you relate: being overscheduled, overcaffeinated, a perfectionist, having too much stuff, or not being well organized? Share tips with one another.

4. Memorize Ephesians 2:8–10. Discuss what these verses mean for you and your children.

BETWEEN YOU AND GOD—PRINCIPLE TO REMEMBER

I defuse the land mine of "mommy meltdowns" by
keeping my mind focused on Christ and His plans for my life.

Father, thank You that You not only saved me but also prepared good works for my children and me to do. Help me to learn what those are and to protect my time so I can fully serve You. Help me to model a balanced life for my children. In Jesus' name, amen.

LAUGH OUT LOUD

God has blessed me by allowing me to teach the three year old Sunday school class for seven years. This year the boys out number the girls 4 to 1 and all are outgoing. Ben, our talker, always has something to say and doesn't mind interrupting to share very loudly. His best buddy Mark chimes in and soon they try to outdo each another. One Sunday as I attempted to tell the Bible story, Ben began to talk. My efforts to redirect him were to no avail. Soon Mark chimed in. Then Jacob decided he needed to make some noise. Needless to say, I became flustered...when sweet little Chad looked at me and said ,"Ms. Janice, we should just have the prayer." Ah....the wisdom of a 3 year old!—Janice Kubica

18

THROWING MY HANDS IN THE AIR OR LIFTING MY CHILD IN PRAYER

I defuse the land mine of throwing my hands in the air in
despair by lifting my child to the Lord in prayer.

Pray without ceasing.

1 Thessalonians 5:17

Toddler Holly picked up the television remote. Her mother offered a trade: "Holly, here's your TV remote that you can play with. That one is mommy's." No use. With a twinkle in her eye, Holly pushed the buttons on the remote that she knew was a no-no. "Holly, no," mother said sternly. "You cannot play with the remote. Here is your remote," she repeated. Lifting Holly into her arms, she dislodged the gadget from her little hands and placed it on a shelf out of Holly's reach. That's when everything broke loose. Holly went into a full-fledged temper tantrum. Mom set Holly on the floor and walked away so the toddler wouldn't have the satisfaction of an audience for her performance.

Later in the day, Mom ventured with ten-year-old Ben and Holly to Target. "Mommy just needs to pick up a few things. We won't be here long. Then, when we get home, we'll have yogurt." In the checkout line, feeling confident that she was going to be able to make it out of the store without a scene, Mom smiled at the cashier. Then it happened. "Candy!" Holly pointed. "We'll have yogurt when we get home, Holly. Do you want some yogurt?" Mom replied. "Candy. Candy! Candy!!!!" Holly screamed, wiggling wildly in the shopping-cart seat, reaching and flailing with both arms for the candy. "Would you like to apply for a credit card today? You can get 10 percent off today's purchase," the cashier asked while Mom tried to control Holly and Ben hid his face in the magazines. Mom, struggling with Holly, replied above her wails: "I can't apply for a credit card right now. I have my hands full." Then, turning to her daughter: "Holly! Settle down RIGHT NOW!"

Where the Rubber Meets the Road

Have you been there? If you're a mom, you may be trying your very best but to what seems like no avail. You may be doing everything you know to do and what you've heard the experts say to do. When nothing works, it's easy to feel like a failure or to wonder if your child is ever going to behave "like other children."

First, please know that all those other children don't behave perfectly. And, second, there are no perfect mommies or children. We each do our best. But what helps and equips us to do our best?

Read and apply what you learn

You are to be commended for reading this book and learning about some potential land mines of parenting and the positive choices you can make. Apply what you're learning. Go back and reread chapters that are especially applicable. Then, read some more. You'll find other recommended resources in the appendix. Take the time to read not just about the current stage you're in with your child but also the next one, so you're better prepared. Ask Christian moms about books and resources that have helped them.

Consider others' advice

I'm not suggesting that you take to heart all the advice you receive but rather that you consider advice in light of God's Word. For instance, if your mother-in-law quips, "A good ole spanking wouldn't hurt," you may want to blow up at her insinuation that you're spoiling your child because you use time-outs. Instead, you may want to consider what Christian authorities say on the subject. Is it possible a smack on Carrie's hand may work more effectively than time-out to teach her not to run into the street?

Pray specifically

When Taylor and Lauren were little, I found it especially helpful to read disciplinary books by Christian authors. Talking to other parents whom I respected and who were raising their children to know the Lord was also a big help. However, the most help I received was in prayer—both by asking God for help and by listening to His answers.

You may think it a small thing and discount the value of praying at all times and asking God for everything. You may have been raised not to bother God with the small stuff. However, nothing could be further from what the Bible teaches. The Bible shows us God and Jesus being involved in the day-to-day lives of people. We have seen through our study in this book that the moms who "did it right" were in communion with God. The moms who went off on their own ended up messing things up for themselves and their children. The fact is, there is an invisible realm that we cannot see with our earthly eyes. In that realm a war rages between God's angels and satanic powers. Satan wants to claim you if you are not a Christian. If you are, he wants to make you live a defeated and depressed life, wounded and out of commission for God's kingdom. Satan wants your child. He will lure your son or daughter through movies, sexting, chat rooms, porn sites, alcohol, drugs, sex, television, and games. He'll sneak into your home through what appears to be harmless. So nothing is beyond God's concern for your child. Nothing is too small for you to talk to Him about and get advice. God is there for you. You would be remiss *not* to talk to Him. So let's go to Him about our kids. Here's just a sampling:

Toddler Carrie hits.

"Lord, You are the God of peace. Jesus is the Prince of Peace. Blanket Carrie with Your peace today. Fill her little heart and mind with peace. Fill me with Your peace so I can discipline her in a way that helps her to know and love You. Help me to teach her to use words to express her feelings rather than to act out by hitting."

Ben is overly shy.

"Lord, You are a God who sees and cares. You see people and are compassionate toward them. Help me teach Ben to see and care for others rather than be inwardly focused and self-conscious. Point me to examples in the Bible to show him how You cared for others."

Mindy won't eat anything but junk food.

"Lord, You created us and the foods to provide for our health. Forgive me for being slack and letting Mindy fill up on chips and cookies. Help me turn our habits around. Help me not to give in to her whining. Develop in her a taste for fruits and vegetables."

Austin plays too roughly.

"Lord, You are kind. Austin's dad is raising him to be "all boy" and plays roughly with him. But now Austin runs roughshod over other children. He's insensitive to them and how they want to play. I'm afraid he's becoming a bully. He's not kind. Help! What should I do?"

Now, praying mom, listen. I hope you have your Bible out and a journal and pen handy to write down how God directs you. It might be something like the following.

Play is play on the football field, but knocking down someone or pushing him down because you feel like it is unkind. So is knocking down someone's Lego tower. Ephesians 4:32 says we are to be kind to one another. Teach Austin, "God is kind." Or, if he's old enough, teach him the first part of the verse: "Be kind one to another, tender-hearted." Show him the verse in the Bible. Let him highlight or color it in yellow in his Bible. Pray over Austin, "Lord, You are kind. Help Austin to be kind like You." Explain to Austin that you'll help him develop kindness by pointing out to him when he isn't. You're on his side, trying to help him establish new habits.

Sometimes, in our family, we invented silly code words to use when we were working on changing habits. For instance, if someone said, "mishemo" in our family, that meant to back off—you were being mean, the teasing was going too far, the joke wasn't funny to that person, or you were hurting someone's feelings. Any one of us had permission to say "mishemo" to another person. Because it was a made-up word, we could say it in public and the person could back off without being disciplined in front of their friends. God will help you come up with creative ideas to help develop your child's character when you go to Him in prayer.

Teenage Amber doesn't like that she can't go to a certain party. She slams her bedroom door while yelling, "You're stupid!"

Our kids would have been too afraid to call us stupid. Had they done so, two things would have happened immediately: prayer and discipline. "God, give me grace, and give Amber a repentant heart" would have been followed with a firm conversation.

"Amber, I know you're angry, but slamming the door won't change things and isn't permitted. You know I love you, but Carol's parents aren't going to be home this weekend, and you know our rule. You are more than welcome to invite friends here. We can order pizza and rent a movie. Or you can go to a movie. In any event, I will not tolerate disrespect. If you act this way, you will be grounded."

Then get on your knees in prayer. "Lord, thank You for loving Amber. Help her to know how much I love her. Calm her heart. In Jesus' name, amen."

If Amber slams the door again, explain: "If you can't control yourself and properly close the door, you'll not have friends over or go anywhere this weekend" (or whatever discipline works with Amber). You may need to help her learn how to diffuse her anger. "Amber, I know sometimes you're really mad. But slamming the door and speak rudely to me is not appropriate. Punch a pillow if you must. Cry out to God in your anger. Speak to Him about what's on your heart. Talk to me. But use a proper tone of voice, and don't destroy our home. I love you. Let me pray for you right now."

Teen Mark drinks and drives.

Children should know there will be serious and swift consequences if they drink and drive. If your child is not of driving age, I suggest that before keys are ever placed in his or her hands, you sit down and have a serious, eye-to-eye discussion. Explain to your children that they are expected to obey the laws and use utmost care in driving; that if they ever violate the law or your trust, you will immediately take their keys and revoke privileges. Pray over your kids when they get their driver's license, entrusting them to God and praying they be cautious, responsible drivers.

For teen Mark, who has driven while drunk, you might pray: "God, You are a loving God who cares for Mark and others. Convict him for the wrong he did in endangering his and others' lives; in violating the civil law and our trust; in violating Your law not to get drunk. Help Mark to develop new friendships with people who won't encourage drinking. Help him to be a strong witness and a leader who says no to what is wrong. Develop his self-control."

Tween Lucy is negative and always sees the glass half full.

"I don't have any friends. No one likes me. And when I don't make the basketball team, I won't have anything to do. I hate school. Everyone makes better grades than me. I want to be in choir, but I know I won't make it. This is going to be a horrible school year."

It's normal for our children to feel down at times, even pessimistic. However, we don't want to ignore negative self-talk. The Bible is clear that we are to think on that which is true, honorable, right, pure, lovely—if there is any excellence, anything worthy of praise, we are to think on those things (Philippians 4:8). In addition, we're to take our thoughts captive to Christ. This is a perfect opportunity for you to train Lucy in God's ways and pray for her.

"Lucy, do you know how much I love you? I'm so sorry that you're feeling down. Sometimes I feel down too, but do you know what really helps? It helps to remember how much God loves us and that He's here for us. It also helps to check our thoughts. As a matter of fact, the Bible tells us to do that. God doesn't want us to stay down in the dumps. Get your Bible—I want to show you something." Ask her to find 2 Corinthians 10:5 and Philippians 4:8–9 and read them. Ask, "Is it true that you don't have any friends?" More than likely, Lucy will be honest and say something like, "Well, Becca and I sit together at lunch. She's kinda nice."

"Okay, good. We'll have Becca over one day after school. Would you like that? Now, about basketball and choir, do you know for a fact that you won't make them?" Again, Lucy will likely acknowledge it's not a fact but more her fear. Point out that if she doesn't make them, there are numerous other activities she can join. Continue helping her get to the bottom of her negative feelings: "Lucy, you said you hate school. Do you really, or are you just worried about your classes?"

Lucy's spouting off a mouthful of negativity isn't something to ignore. Nor will it be helped by an irritated reply such as, "Oh, hush Lucy. I'm sick of you're being so negative! Go do your homework," or a shallow, "Cheer up!"

Windows of Opportunity

Our children's needs are an opportunity to develop their spirits. Children are spiritual beings with the need for spiritual guidance. The truth is found in the Bible, and the empowerment to perform it is found through prayer. Model for your kids the practice of looking to the Bible for truth and to God for power. Talk to them in gentleness and with reason from the time they are young, and it won't seem weird as they grow older. It will be a continuation of your fulfilling your responsibility to train your children as you go about your day.

If I could recommend one thing regarding training your children and teaching them about God, it's this: keep it short and simple. Don't cram things down their throats or be legalistic. Show mercy and grace, even as God extends it to you. Don't expect, after telling your kids something once and praying for them, that they will be bouncy, happy, perfect children. God has been working on you and me for years, and we're not perfect. Christ continues to intercede for us, and God disciplines and forgives us. Do likewise with your children. State the consequences of disobedience, then follow through in love, not anger. Let praying for your children be natural to their ears.

Following, a friend shares how God led her to pray for her child rather than simply throw her hands in the air in despair.

When I was a young mother, a friend told me she was already praying for her children's spouses. I remember thinking, "My prayer list is loaded with prayers for potty training, sleeping through the night, a temper-tantrum-free day, time with my husband, etc. How could I even think about praying for a someday spouse for my four children under the age of ten?"

But God placed on my heart it was something I needed to pray about, even if it wouldn't occur for twenty years. Over time, prayers for potty training changed to prayers for doing well on spelling tests, making a cheering squad, getting accepted to the university of their dreams, and finding a successful career path. But one prayer never changed: "Send my children godly men and women who will honor them forever."

When our oldest daughter graduated from the University of Texas and was working in Austin, she met a young man she believed was "the one." Unfortunately, when my husband and I met him, we were not impressed. He claimed to be a Christian but rarely attended church and seemed immature, and I felt he didn't honor our daughter in the way I would expect a man to behave when he's truly in love and wants to spend his life with her. I tried to engage him in conversation, but each time, his comments seemed shallow and caused me more concern. My husband and I were honest with Leah about our concerns, but she insisted he was right for her. Their relationship lasted more than two years. I was in panic mode, but whenever the panic started to overwhelm me, I went to God and said, "Father,

I believe You will send Leah the man You have in mind for her. If this is him, please reveal to me what it is that she loves so much about him so that I can love him too."

In April, Leah was transferred to Dallas. Though it was difficult for her to leave her boyfriend, she knew it was a good career and financial move. Within a few months, their relationship became strained, and she shared with me that she was frustrated and confused. I dedicated the next several days to praying for my daughter and her future; praying specifically for God to give her wisdom, understanding, right judgment, courage, knowledge, and reverence for Him.

At the end of nine days, God placed on my heart that I should mail a prayer booklet that I was using to Leah. My husband and I were leaving on a trip that day, and I had so many last-minute arrangements to make, but I obeyed God's prompting and took the time to mail it to her. Little did I know that Leah and her boyfriend would have a huge disagreement and break up that night.

Plan A Mom Tip

Be proactive in your prayers for your children. Teach them God's character, then use His character as the springboard for your prayers for your children. (An example is provided in the appendix of this book: *365 A–Z Names, Titles, and Attributes of God.*[1])

Three days later, the prayer booklet arrived in Leah's mailbox—the same day her boyfriend called to try to patch things up. She told him about the prayer booklet and said she was going to dedicate the next few days to prayer and not to call her during that time. She didn't share with me all the details that God revealed to her in those days of prayer, but one thing was made clear to her: she needed to end the relationship with her boyfriend.

I praise God for His Spirit and the gifts He bestows on us when we ask for them. God gave Leah wisdom and knowledge to look honestly at her relationship with this young man. He gave her right judgment and courage. If Leah told this story, it might have a different twist, but one thing would be the same: God hears the cries of His people and leads us by His Spirit to His perfect plan. I will continue to pray for the right spouse for my children, even if it takes another twenty years!

LIVE OUT LOUD

Plan A Mom Checkup

1. When frustrated, do you typically just get upset and go on about your day? Or do you carve out time to pray about the parenting challenge that is causing you and your child despair?
2. Do you pray general, "be with my child" prayers? Or do you also pray specifically for your child?
3. Do you take advantage of teachable moments and point your children to God's truths, then pray for them in their presence?

LOVE OUT LOUD

1. What can you take home and apply from this chapter?
2. What kinds of specific things do you pray for your children?
3. Give an example of a teachable moment with your child, what passage of Scripture you used, and how you prayed for him or her.
4. What did you learn from the mom's testimony of praying for her daughter?
5. Describe what you understand to be the difference between cramming God's Word down your child's throat and speaking the truth in love and praying.
6. What do you feel your heavenly Father is trying to teach you, His child?

BETWEEN YOU AND GOD—PRINCIPLE TO REMEMBER

I defuse the land mine of throwing my hands in
the air in despair by lifting my child to the Lord in prayer.

Heavenly Father, You're such an incredible parent to me. I'm awed by Your patience, grace, and love. Help me to discipline my child in love, as You discipline me. Help me establish wise parameters and model in my own life what I expect of them. Help my children to know that my arms of love are ever extended to them. In Jesus' name, amen.

LAUGH OUT LOUD

One of my favorite parenting stories came from an early lesson on the Golden Rule. Our son Chris and daughter Carrie were very young and had been picking on each other. I sat them down and talked to them about treating other people, not the way they treat you, but how you want to be treated. They both seemed to understand, and I was pleased that I had conquered sibling rivalry. For about twenty-five seconds. Then Carrie came running to me, crying that Chris had hit her. I said, "Chris, why did you hit your sister? Didn't we just talk about the Golden Rule?" He replied, "Yes, and then she hit me, so I figured she was treating me like she wanted to be treated, and I hit her back."—Lynn Hokanson

Appendix A

75 Pointers for a Sane Family

1. Always say "I love you" when you part for the day.
2. Apologize if you do something wrong.
3. Attend church together.
4. Be in the moment with the person you're with rather than thinking about something else.
5. Be responsible. If you say you're going to do something, do it.
6. Be kind to one another.
7. Be willing to go out of your way for others.
8. Compliment one another.
9. Celebrate birthdays and achievements.
10. Call if you're going to be late.
11. Do your homework and chores.
12. Don't go to bed angry. Agree, if need be, to continue to discuss differences of opinion the next day; but affirm your love for each other before saying good night.
13. Don't expect others to be perfect; you're not.
14. Don't be bossy, demand your way all the time, or insist on having the last word.
15. Eat together as a family.
16. Eat to be healthy.
17. Exercise . . . at least walk. Anything is better than nothing.
18. Everyone has chores; do yours.
19. Forgive as God has forgiven you.
20. Garbage in, garbage out: be careful what you let in.
21. Greet each other when you come home and ask about each other's day.
22. Have morning devotions as a family.
23. Hold one another accountable—in love.

24. If someone wrongs you, don't hold a grudge. Address it with the person sooner, not later, after first prayerfully checking your own heart.
25. If a family member is hurting your feelings or being mean, use a family code word to alert him or her to stop.
26. If you break something, apologize and make amends.
27. Just say no to wrong behavior.
28. Keep your word.
29. Love one another, and express your love verbally and in how you treat each other.
30. Let someone know where you are.
31. Look one another in the eye when you are talking.
32. Laugh together. Telling old stories keeps them alive in your mind.
33. Love and forgive as you are loved and forgiven.
34. Learn to distinguish between the Spirit and the flesh so you can yield to the Spirit.
35. Listen to Christian music to lift your spirits.
36. Listen when someone is talking to you
37. Learn to make conversation. Ask questions. Be interested in people, not just absorbed in yourself.
38. Major in the majors, and minor in the minors.
39. Never hang up on one another. Always say good-bye.
40. Never leave the house mad at one another.
41. No television in children's bedrooms.
42. No hitting, pushing, shoving, bad language, or disrespectful behavior.
43. Obey immediately. Slow obedience is no obedience.
44. Open the door for one another.
45. Pray together and for one another's needs.
46. Pick up after yourself.
47. Put God first, family second, work third.
48. Play together: water ski, play board games, go to sporting events, etc.
49. Quickly make up after disagreements.
50. Read the Bible and good books.
51. Respect each other's privacy and differences.

52. Remember that you don't have to buy everything right when you see it or want it.

53. Return what you borrow.

54. Respond to needs for a ride or to deliver a forgotten wallet.

55. Say good morning.

56. Say, "Good night, I love you" before going to bed.

57. Say yes and no sir and ma'am, please and thank you.

58. Set your alarm rather than depending on someone to wake you.

59. Support each other's activities.

60. Tell the truth, even if you have to suffer the consequences. Never lie.

61. Thank the person who prepared or purchased your meal or did something to help you.

62. Take your Bible to church so you can follow the teaching.

63. Tithe. Save. Spend some on what you want or need.

64. Thank God for your meals.

65. Take pictures, even if someone is going through a nonsmiling stage.

66. Take care of aging parents.

67. Take turns.

68. Take your plate to the sink, rinse it, and put it in the dishwasher.

69. Use a parent for an excuse to say no to something you don't want to do if the peer pressure is too great for you to stand against it by yourself.

70. Vacation together.

71. When you work, work hard. When you play, play hard.

72. Wait up for your children to come home at night, or wake up when they arrive.

73. Watch shows and movies that build up rather than tear down godly character.

74. Expect the best of each other.

75. Zealously seek the Lord individually and as a family.

APPENDIX B

365 A–Z Names, Titles, and Attributes of God

Proverbs 18:10 says, "The name of the Lord is a strong tower; the righteous runs into it and is safe." Paul said, in Philippians 3:7–10, that his desire was to know Christ and the power of His resurrection. These verses summarize my passion: to know Christ and the power of His resurrection and to help others know Him and His power. Only then can we stand against the enemy and glorify the One who so loved us that He gave His life that we might be saved.

I invite you to join me in raising the next generation to know Christ and His power. Following is a sample from *365 A–Z Names, Titles, and Attributes of God*.[1] Each morning, use one of the attributes for your devotions with your children, or e-mail one to your teen or adult child. Upon completing each one, check or date the box. If you skip a day, you can catch up the next day; or even spend Saturday morning allowing each family member to pick an attribute and share why it's important to him or her. You might also use bedtime to let your children find a name or attribute in their Bibles. Encourage your kids to underline or circle each attribute in their Bible—perhaps in purple to remind them of God's royalty. A Bible with 365 circled attributes serves a mom and child well when Plan B comes along.

You can also use the attribute as a springboard when you P.R.A.Y. (Praise, Repent, Ask, and Yield[2] and teach your children to pray. For instance, let's take Abba Father. Read the verse(s) and talk about how wonderful it is that God is our daddy in heaven. He's adopted us. He loves us very much. We're important to Him. We can ask Him anything, talk to Him about anything. He has gifts for us, a rich inheritance. (The depth to which you go should depend on the age and maturity of the child.) Then P.R.A.Y.:

- *Praise.* "God, we praise You for being our Abba Father.
- *Repent.* "Forgive us when we forget how much You love us and when we disobey.

- *Ask.* "Help us to act and talk like Your children today.
- *Yield.* "Fill our minds and hearts with Your thoughts.

☐ Abba Father	Romans 8:15; Galatians 4:6
☐ Abides Forever	Psalm 9:7
☐ Abolisher of Death	2 Timothy 1:10
☐ Above All	Ephesians 1:21
☐ Advocate	1 John 2:1
☐ All Powerful (Omnipotent)	Matthew 28:18; Revelation 19:6
☐ Almighty God	Genesis 17:1–2; Psalm 91:1–2
☐ Alpha and Omega	Revelation 1:8; 22:13
☐ Amazing	Matthew 7:28; Mark 1:22; Luke 2:47
☐ Anchor of My Soul	Hebrews 6:19
☐ Anointed One	Psalm 2:2; Luke 4:18
☐ Apostle and High Priest	Hebrews 3:1
☐ Author and Perfecter of My Faith	Hebrews 12:2
☐ Awesome	Deuteronomy 7:21; Nehemiah 1:5

For more information and suggestions, see *Pray with Purpose, Live with Passion* and the *Prayers of My Heart* prayer journal. For younger children, use *Kidz Time 2: Praising God A to Z.*

MORE RESOURCES BY
DEBBIE TAYLOR WILLIAMS

The Plan A Woman in a Plan B World
Pray with Purpose, Live with Passion
Prayers of My Heart prayer journal
If God is in Control, Why Am I a Basket Case?
If God is in Control, Why Do I Have a Headache?
Discovering His Passion
365 A–Z Names, Titles, and Attributes of God
Kidz Time 1: Bible Verses A to Z
Kidz Time 2: Praising God A to Z
Trusting God's People . . . Again (Blake Coffee and Debbie Taylor Williams)

Recommended Reading
Boundaries with Kids, Dr. Henry Cloud and Dr. John Townsend
Bringing Up Kids without Tearing Them Down, Dr. Kevin Leman
It's Okay, God, We Can Take It, Bo Neuhaus with Lindy Neuhaus
Ordering Your Private World, Gordon MacDonald
Praying for Your Prodigal Daughter, Janet Thompson
Raising Respectful Children in a Disrespectful World, Jill M. Rigby
The Power of a Positive Mom, Karol Ladd
The Strong-Willed Child, Dr. James Dobson

Helpful Links
Crosswalk Parenting: www.crosswalk.com/parenting
Focus on the Family Movie Reviews: www.pluggedinonline.com
Focus on the Family Parenting: http://www.focusonthefamily.com/parenting.aspx
Family Talk with Dr. James Dobson: http://www.myfamilytalk.com/articles-parenting.aspx
Family Life Today: http://www.familylife.com/site/c.dnJHKLNnFoG/b.6235823/k.809F/FamilyLife_Today.htm?utm_source=redirect&utm_medium=flt-dot-com&utm_campaign=flt
Mops International: http://www.mops.org

Notes

Chapter 1

1 *Merriam-Webster's Collegiate Dictionary*, 10th ed., s.v. "snot."
2 *Strong's Exhaustive Concordance of the Bible*, electronic ed., H3707.
3 Ibid., G3949.
4 Debbie Taylor Williams, *The Plan A Woman in a Plan B World* (Abilene, TX: Leafwood, 2010). Visit Debbie's Web site at www.debbiewilliams.com.

Chapter 2

1 *Strong's*, H819.
2 Ibid., H5771.
3 Ibid., G1777.
4 Ibid., G5485.
5 Ibid., G5485.

Chapter 3

1 Ibid., H553.
2 Zig Ziglar, "Attitude Makes All the Difference," http://itunes.apple.com/us/podcast/inspiring-words-encouragement/id192820274, number 129, 8/21/07.
3 *Strong's*, G2170.
4 Gary Hill, ed., *The Discovery Bible, New American Standard New Testament Reference Edition* (Chicago: Moody Press, 1987) xv, 402, and "Key to Discovery Symbols" (inside back cover).
5 *Merriam-Webster's Collegiate Dictionary*, s.v. "attitude."
6 Ibid., s.v. "gratitude."
7 Debbie Taylor Williams, *365 A–Z Names, Titles, and Attributes of God* (Kerrville, TX: Hill Country Ministries, 2010).

Chapter 4

1 *Merriam-Webster's Collegiate Dictionary*, s.v. "manipulate."
2 *Strong's*, H8535.
3 *Strong's*, H5889.
4 *Merriam-Webster's Collegiate Dictionary*, s.v. "preempt."

Chapter 5

1 *Strong's*, ??.
2 *The Holy Bible: New International Version* (Grand Rapids, MI: Zondervan, 1996, 1984).
3 Pam Kanaly is the author of *Will the Real Me Please Stand Up* (Mustang, OK: Tate Publishing Company, 2007).

Chapter 6

1 *Strong's*, H7043.
2 *The Holy Bible: The Good News Translation*, 2nd ed. (New York: American Bible Society, 1992).
3 *Strong's*, H3045.
4 Thelma Wells, http://www.thelmawells.com/.

Chapter 7

1 *Strong's*, H1961.
2 Williams, *365 A–Z Names, Titles, and Attributes of God*.

3 Debbie Williams, *Pray with Purpose, Live with Passion* (West Monroe, LA: Howard Books, 2006) and P.R.A.Y. with Purpose Across the Nation Conference, http://debbietaylorwilliams.com/pray-conference/.
4 *Strong's*, H8150.
5 Kamal Saleem, *The Blood of the Lambs* (New York: Howard Books, 2009), 9–11.
6 Ibid., 22.
7 "Fetal Development," National Right to Life, http://www.nrlc.org/abortion/facts/fetaldevelopment.html
8 Debbie Taylor Williams, *Kidz Time 1: Bible Verses A to Z* (Kerrville, TX: Hill Country Ministries, 1999).

Chapter 11

1 *Merriam-Webster's Collegiate Dictionary*, s.v. "prodigal."
2 Herbert Lockyer, *All the Women of the Bible* (Grand Rapids, MI: Zondervan, 1988), 80.
3 Adapted excerpts from Janet Thompson's *Praying for Your Prodigal Daughter: Hope, Help & Encouragement for Hurting Parents* (New York: Howard Books, 2008). Visit Janet's Web site at www.womantowomanmentoring.com.

Chapter 12

1 *Strong's*, H1361.

Chapter 13

1 Ibid., G1553.
2 Ibid., G548.
3 Bo Neuhaus with Lindy Neuhaus, *It's Okay, God, We Can Take It* (Austin, TX: Diamond Books, 1986), 8.
4 Ibid., 12–13.
5 Ibid., 98.
6 *Strong's*, G5242.

Chapter 14

1 Ibid., G4933.
2 Ibid., G1301.
3 Dena Dyer is a Texas-born-and-raised wife and mom who loves to encourage women through writing, speaking, blogging, and singing. She's the author of several books, hundreds of articles, and dozens of essays. Find out more by visiting her blog, "Mother Inferior," at http://www.denadyer.typepad.com.

Chapter 15

1 Williams, *365 A–Z Names, Titles, and Attributes of God*.

Chapter 16

1 Debbie Taylor Williams, *If God Is in Control, Why Do I Have a Headache?* (Birmingham, AL: New Hope Publishers, 2004).

Chapter 17

1 Lockyer, *All the Women of the Bible*, 169.

Chapter 18

1 Williams, *365 A–Z Names, Titles, and Attributes of God*.

Chapter 19

1 Ibid.
2 Williams, *Pray with Purpose, Live with Passion*.

About the Author

Debbie Taylor Williams, founder of Hill Country Ministries, whose mission is to spread God's Word and love, is a sought-after national Christian speaker and author. Best known as a passionate Bible expositor, Debbie uses humor and practical illustrations to communicate spiritual truths to women throughout the nation. She has written and produced numerous books and video-driven Bible studies, including *The Plan A Woman in a Plan B World*; *Pray with Purpose, Live with Passion*; *Prayers of My Heart*; *If God Is in Control, Why Do I Have a Headache?*; *If God Is in Control, Why Am I a Basket Case?*; and *Discovering His Passion*. She also coauthored *Trusting God's People . . . Again*. In addition, she has been published in *P31 Woman* magazine and is a religion columnist for the *Kerrville Daily Times*. Debbie is currently taking her conference, P.R.A.Y. with Passion, across the nation.

Debbie and Keith, her husband of more than thirty-five years, live in Kerrville, Texas. They are blessed with two married children and one grandson. Debbie's spiritual investment in others was acknowledged when she was recognized as Kerrville's 2000 Woman of the Year.

To invite Debbie to speak or for more information about her books or conferences, visit her Web site at www.debbietaylorwilliams.com or call (888) 815-9412.

Also by Debbie Taylor Williams

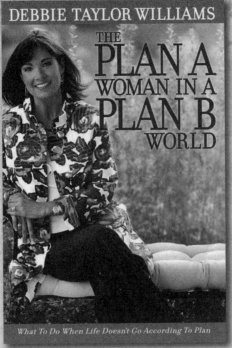

ISBN 978-0-89112-641-6 | 224 pages | $14.99

"Debbie Williams will engage your heart, mind, and funny bone. She reminds us that when our stories play out differently than we would've written them, our Creator Redeemer is still in control."

— LISA HARPER, Women of Faith speaker and author of *A Perfect Mess*

"I've been in women's ministry for years and never have I been more convinced of the need for a book like this. Thousands of women will discover how they can live with Christ-centered purpose and victory in spite of a major life disappointment."

— PAM KANALY, author of *Will the Real Me Please Stand Up*

"Debbie Williams has captured the heartbeat of every woman .... You won't be able to put this book down. Be prepared to be transformed."

— HEIDI McLAUGHLIN, author of *Beauty Unleashed: Transforming a Woman's Soul*

Ask for it at your favorite bookstore
Or contact Leafwood Publishers

www.leafwoodpublishers.com
877-816-4455 toll free